THE COMPLETE GUIDE TO THE MUSIC OF

pink floyd

_Y ANDY MABBETT

Copyright © 1995 Omnibus Press (A Division of Book Sales Limited)

Edited by Chris Charlesworth
Cover & Book designed by 4i Limited
Picture research by Nikki Russell

ISBN: 0.7119.4301.X Order No: OP 47735

Exclusive Distributors
Book Sales Limited, 8/9 Frith Street, London W1V 5TZ, UK.
Music Sales Corporation, 257 Park Avenue South, New York, NY 10010, USA.
Music Sales Pty Limited, 120 Rothschild Avenue, Rosebery, NSW 2018, Australia.

To the Music Trade only:
Music Sales Limited, 8/9 Frith Street, London W1V 5TZ, UK.

Photo credits:
Rex Features: front cover; Barry Plummer: back cover; all other photos supplied by LFI, Barry Plummer, Retna & Rex Features.

Every effort has been made to trace the copyright holders of the photographs in this book but one or
two were unreachable. We would be grateful if the photographers concerned would contact us.

Printed in Great Britain by Printwise (Haverhill) Limited.

A catalogue record for this book is available from the British Library.

contents

introduction

From their beginnings as an improvising, blues-based psychedelic band with hit pop singles to a period when every other journalist insisted, mistakenly, in describing them as "electronic rockers"; from the ubiquitous 'Dark Side Of The Moon' to being the first rock band played in space; from losing not one, but two key members to performing a two-hundred date stadium tour; from an underwear thief and 'Several Species Of Small Furry Creatures Gathered Together In A Cave And Grooving With A Pict' to the doom and gloom of 'The Wall', Pink Floyd have always been bigger, better and braver than the rest.

As pioneering users of stage lighting, quadrophonic concerts, theatrical stage shows and a hundred and one technical and artistic innovations, the band have never accepted the words "can't be done" from their collaborators. Such eagerness to embrace the new would be empty bravado, were it not matched with thoughtful, meaningful lyrics and stories, exquisite musicianship and, not least, damn fine tunes. That's not to say there haven't been lapses; as we shall see, they have had their share of turkeys; but even these have been produced with style.

David Gilmour, Syd Barrett and Roger Waters (and, indeed, several other people who will crop up as the story unfolds) all knew each other from their school days in the early Sixties in Cambridge. While Gilmour spent his late teenage years busking and gigging in France and Northern Spain, Barrett attended college in Cambridge and Waters studied in London, where he met fellow architecture students Nick Mason, son of a well-known director of motoring films, and Rick Wright, a part-trained classical musician with jazz tendencies. They formed a series of groups, eventually bringing in Barrett (who was also now in London, his artistic talents having earned him a place on a painting course). These short-lived bands went under various names, including The Meggadeaths, Sigma 6, The (Architectural) Abdabs, Leonard's Lodgers and The T-Set, before settling on the name The Pink Floyd Sound, which as every Seventies schoolboy knew, was taken from two of Syd Barrett's favourite bluesmen, Pink Anderson and Floyd Council. As their confidence grew, they went from pop and R&B covers to their own extended psychedelic improvisations, loved by the "freaks" of the emerging underground movement in London but hated by straighter concert goers everywhere else.

What subsequently gave the band such a large and loyal following, and kept the albums selling in phenomenal quantities, was a combination of factors – the innovations, the attention to small detail and quality, the superb music, the cleverness of Waters' concepts and their relevance to everyday life, the mystery that grew around their reluctance to be photographed or interviewed for much of the Seventies, the lack of singles during the same crucial period, the imaginative album packaging, the crisp live sound, the spectacular theatrical shows – and, of course, a special magic that cannot be copied no matter how much money or equipment is available.

Enough of the band's history is included in this book to allow the reader to make sense of the background to their recordings. For a more complete view, readers are referred to *Crazy Diamond – Syd Barrett and The Dawn Of Pink Floyd* by Mike Watkinson & Pete Anderson and *Pink Floyd - A Visual Documentary* by Miles and myself. Both titles are published by Omnibus Press. The other two essential Pink Floyd biographies are *Bricks In The Wall* by Karl Dallas (Baton Press, 1987, but re-published in America in 1994 with a shamefully inaccurate, ghost-written update) and the late Nick Schaffner's *Saucerful Of Secrets* (Sidgwick & Jackson, 1991). Internet users should also subscribe to "alt.music.pink-floyd" and "alt.music.roger-waters".

Reference is made throughout the first half of this book to the band's BBC *In-Concert* recordings and sessions. The former originally took the form of shows performed in the BBC's Paris Theatre, London and recorded for later broadcast, although these days they tend to be recorded, or broadcast live, from any suitable venue on a band's itinerary. The sessions are a different beast. Bands have, since before Radio One's creation in 1967, used the BBC's

studios to record tracks for broadcast, usually reprising recent albums or singles. In a few cases, though, bands have chosen to air new material, perform cover versions (but not in Pink Floyd's case) or try out numbers which were sometimes quietly forgotten. Readers interested in this influential, but often overlooked, aspect of British popular music culture could do worse than read Ken Garner's superb *In Session Tonight* (BBC Books, 1993). Although the band and their management consistently refuse to sanction their official release, most of their sessions are available on good quality bootlegs.

At the time of writing, EMI are about two-thirds of the way through re-releasing all of Pink Floyd's albums as picture-label CDs and cassettes, but not vinyl, using improved digital masters (some from the 'Shine On' box set) and revamped packaging, with full lyrics. Those not already released are scheduled to hit the shops sometime in 1995. Bootleggers also have their own "reissue" plans: in addition to the usual plethora of live material and studio out-takes, they have recently released Orb-style remixes of 'Meddle', 'Dark Side...', 'Wish You Were Here' and 'The Division Bell'. Purists hate them, but the care and humour with which they have been crafted show that the remixers obviously have a deep respect for Pink Floyd.

I must take this opportunity to offer thanks to all contributors to *The Amazing Pudding*, especially my fellow editors Bruno MacDonald, Ivor Trueman and Dave Walker. Adrian Banham and Kev Whitlock have, with Bruno, worked extremely hard, without complaining, to check facts and proof-read texts. Information and assistance has also been freely supplied by Vernon Fitch, Aaro Koskinen, Alain Lachaud, George Loaf, Soraya Patrick, Danni Ryan and all in the EMI and PMI press offices. However, the biggest debt of gratitude is owed to Smaranda, whose patience and understanding have been sorely tried by my obsession with this project.

I've really enjoyed revisiting the band's work while writing this book – over-familiarity had led me to ignore some of the records for far too long. I hope these essays will enable you to hear the records with the same pleasure, whether you're an avid fan wanting in-depth knowledge, or a novice seeking guidance. Pink Floyd are estimated to have sold, world-wide, in the order of 150 million copies of their 18 albums. This is their story...

Andy Mabbett, Birmingham, December 1994

Andy Mabbett was, for ten years, co-editor of *The Amazing Pudding*, the widely-respected Pink Floyd and Roger Waters magazine. He has written about the band for several magazines, including *Q* and *Mojo* and has contributed to *Crazy Diamond – Syd Barrett and The Dawn Of Pink Floyd* and co-authored *Pink Floyd – The Visual Documentary* with Miles. Both are published by Omnibus Press. He currently writes about music for Brum Beat, and non-musical subjects for a range of other publications.

Although *The Amazing Pudding* ceased publication in December 1993, some back issues are still available – for details, please send a SAE (or International Reply Coupon if overseas) to Andy Mabbett c/o 67, Cramlington Road, Great Barr, Birmingham, B42 2EE, England. No phone calls please!

tonite let's all make love in london

See For Miles SEE CD 258; originally Instant INLP 002, released circa 1968

Other than some poor-quality demos made in October 1966, Pink Floyd's first recording session was on 11 and 12 January 1967, in Sound Techniques Studio, London. Syd Barrett's girlfriend persuaded film director Peter Whitehead to fund the sessions, where the band cut two of Barrett's songs, 'Arnold Layne' and 'Let's Roll Another One', and two lengthy instrumental jams, 'Interstellar Overdrive' and 'Nick's Boogie', the latter much closer to their contemporary live performances. Only very short extracts of 'Interstellar Overdrive' were used in Tonite Let's All Make Love In London, the film for which the tracks had been intended, and on the original soundtrack LP.

In 1990, See For Miles Records acquired the original master tape of the two instrumentals, covered in green mould. Fortunately, it was wound so tightly that the playing surface of the tape was unaffected and they were able to release an extended soundtrack album, featuring the short clips of 'Interstellar Overdrive' together with the full 16 3/4 minute version, plus the previously unreleased 'Nick's Boogie'. The two long pieces are also available on an EP (See For Miles SEA CD4) and a poster-sleeve variant (SFM 2). Both the EP and album include (different) dialogue extracts from the film, and the album also has music by other artists.

Four years later, See For Miles released *The Pink Floyd London 1966-67* (PFVP 1), a video comprising both these tracks, set to hitherto unknown footage from the recording session, clips of a Floyd gig at the UFO club, mixed Sixties scenes and film, not of Pink Floyd, shot at the "14 Hour Technicolour Dream" of 29 April 1967, at which they did appear. The original movie, in which Pink Floyd are briefly glimpsed, is also available on video (PFVP 2).

On all these releases, 'Interstellar Overdrive', a group composition, is erroneously credited to Barrett alone, and is a different version from the one released later by EMI. 'Nick's Boogie' is credited as a Pink Floyd composition. All formats are mono.

Since October 1966, the band members had been part of an equal, six-way partnership, Blackhill Publishing, with their managers, Peter Jenner and Andrew King. The latter pair took the two short songs from Whitehead's sessions to EMI subsidiary Columbia, who were sufficiently impressed to sign the band.

the piper at the gates of dawn

EMI 8 31261 2; originally Columbia SCX 6157; first issued on CD as CDP 7 46384 2, released August 5 1967

UK Chart: No. 6; US Chart: n/a

There are those who regard Pink Floyd's début as the band's best album. It is so far removed from 'Dark Side...' and 'The Wall' that it is hard to believe they were recorded by the same band. Indeed, in many ways, they weren't; the manic, erratic, unpredictable and unreliable Syd Barrett was clearly their leader and, unlikely as it may now seem, Rick Wright was the second most dominant force musically. For a record that is every bit as much a product of the swinging Sixties as any of its contemporaries, it is remarkable that 'Piper...' hasn't dated anywhere near as much as its vintage would suggest. No doubt the absence of "Make Love Not War" and drug themes plays a large part in this.

The English whimsy which many attribute to the album is first evident from the title, taken from a chapter in Kenneth Grahame's *Wind In The Willows*, required reading for all Barrett-o-philes.

Barrett, his mental state deteriorating by the day as the pressures of stardom, and no doubt his copious intake of LSD, took their toll, was notoriously difficult to work with,

changing tunes and lyrics between – and during – takes.

The album's producer, Norman Smith, was then best known as the engineer on every Beatles album up to and including 'Rubber Soul', and it was only his work with Pink Floyd that kept him from working on 'Sergeant Pepper', which was being pieced together in an adjacent studio at Abbey Road. At one

point during the sessions Paul McCartney stopped by to listen, and in a subsequent press interview described the Floyd's début album as "a knockout". Much of the technical jiggery pokery which created the sound on 'Piper...' was learned by Smith through his work with The Beatles although, listening to the playout on 'Bike' or the panning on 'Interstellar Overdrive', it's intriguing to think what he would have made of the album had he had access to a modern, digital studio. One quirk of late Sixties recording practices is the simultaneously released mono version (Columbia SC 6157) which is substantially different from the stereo mix we all know and love.

A second Barrett-composed single, 'See Emily Play' is not on the album, but was added to the Japanese release (Toshiba/ EMI EMS 50104), which also had a lyric sheet. It was also on the original US version, available in mono and stereo (Tower T 5093/ ST 5093 respectively), with a different tracklisting: See Emily Play; Pow R Toc H; Take Up Thy Stethoscope & Walk; Lucifer Sam; Matilda Mother; Scarecrow; The Gnome; Chapter 24; Interstellar Overdrive. Later releases in both countries have reverted to the UK tracklisting.

The front cover was an embarrassingly gimmicky group photo, taken with the aid of a multi-image filter. Barrett designed the better, Rorschach inkblot-like group silhouette on the rear of the sleeve. Sadly, this is reduced in prominence, and cropped, on the 1994 re-issue, although the new version does offer vastly improved sound quality and many extra photographs.

'Piper...' was re-released in December 1973, with 'A Saucerful Of Secrets', as one half of the vinyl 'A Nice Pair' package (Harvest SHDW 403), cashing in on the success of 'Dark Side Of The Moon'.

ASTRONOMY DOMINE
(BARRETT)

The first voice heard on the album, reciting the names of astronomical bodies through a megaphone, belongs to Peter Jenner, one of the band's managers. The opening Morse code, said to be gibberish, soon gives way to sweeping organs, echoey guitars and rat-tat-tat drumming, the like of which few listeners could have previously experienced, even in 1967. And is there early evidence of Barrett's paranoia in the lyric "Stars can frighten"?

'Astronomy Domine' was recorded again in 1969, for the live half of 'Ummagumma'. The Canadian version of 'A Nice Pair' manages to use this live cut instead of the original. After it was dropped from the live set in February 1971, Pink Floyd fans the world over expressed great surprise when this Barrett composition was resurrected for Pink Floyd's 1994 tour of America and Europe, oil-slide lights and all, even gaining a second live release, as the B-side of their 'Take It Back' single, performed by the three veteran Floyds with Guy Pratt adding bass.

LUCIFER SAM
(BARRETT)

Partly about Syd's Siamese cat and partly about his girlfriend Jenny, referred to as "Jennifer Gentle" in the lyrics. The "left side/right side" line refers to the division between the logical and creative functions of the respective hemispheres of the brain. Despite the very "Sixties" tone of the guitar and organ, like that on most of the album, the song still sounds fresh and vital today.

MATILDA MOTHER
(BARRETT)

Syd's role-play as a frightened child, not wanting its mother to put out the light after a bedtime story, uses some of his most eloquent and poetic writing. Interestingly, Syd returned to live with his mother when his pop career ended, remaining very close to her until her death in 1991.

Rick Wright's organ provides a typical example of what Peter Jenner christened "one of his Turkish Delight riffs", referring to similarities with an advert for the seductively delicious chocolate bar which was being screened at the time. The song was a favourite concert piece when Syd was in the band, and was recorded for Pink Floyd's first BBC radio session in October 1967.

FLAMING
(BARRETT)

There is a childlike quality in this song also, and of course the line "here we go, ever so high" is completely innocent...

A slightly different mix was released as a single in the USA, despite initially being omitted from the album there.

Another part of the first BBC session, 'Flaming' was performed live by both the Barrett and Gilmour line-ups, where it was sometimes sung by Waters, sometimes by Gilmour. Although it didn't stay in the set list for long, it was performed in November 1969 for a French TV special, "Tous En Scène".

POW R. TOC H.
(BARRETT/WATERS/WRIGHT/MASON)

"Toc H" is a charity, taking its name from army signallers' code for Talbot House, a club house just behind allied lines in World War One, where rank was ignored. Toc H aims to encourage friendships between young people from different backgrounds. Quite what all this noble activity has to do with a group-composed instrumental is not known, nor is the

origin of the "Pow R." half of the title. What is known is that it was recorded for the BBC in December 1967 and survived to become known as 'The Pink Jungle', part of 'The Journey'. There are some differences toward the end of the mono mix.

TAKE UP THY STETHOSCOPE AND WALK
(WATERS)

It is perhaps significant that the only member of the band other than Barrett to have his own song used on the album was Roger Waters, although he later described it as "a very bad song", forgetting his own advice that "music helps to ease the pain". Waters shares the vocals with Barrett, although there aren't very many of them. Indeed, the song shows little indication of the future direction of his writing.

INTERSTELLAR OVERDRIVE
(BARRETT/WATERS/WRIGHT/MASON)

Pink Floyd had already recorded two versions of this lengthy instrumental jam (probably the closest they came on record to the wild improvisations of their then live performances) before signing to EMI. The first was one of the

tracks recorded during their first, unissued, demo recordings, the other for *Tonite Let's All Make Love In London*, detailed above. When it came to recording the track for 'Piper…', therefore, they were already quietly confident to be going out on such a radical limb.

The main theme evolved from Syd's jam around the riff from Love's 'My Little Red Book', as hummed to him by manager Peter Jenner. One persistent, if unlikely, fallacy is that the riff was lifted from the theme to the TV comedy, "Steptoe And Son".

The wild stereo panning is the work of Norman Smith, the band following the trend set by The Beatles, of working on the mono mix of the album and leaving the stereo version to studio boffins, the differences between the two versions being most noticeable at the end of the track.

A rendition for the BBC session of December '68 showed that David Gilmour was just as capable of psychedelic wackiness as Barrett. An historic performance at the October '69 Amougies Pop & Jazz festival, in Belgium, was honoured by Frank Zappa jamming with the band. For 'The Journey', its middle section was used as 'The Labyrinths of

Auximines', although the track was also performed in its own right until well into 1970. In 1971, the 'Piper...' version reappeared on the RELICS compilation.

THE GNOME
(BARRETT)

Almost a straight nursery song, Barrett's tale of the little folk is enhanced by Wright's celeste backing – hardly a Rock 'n' Roll instrument, but ideally suited to the task. This song, too, was recorded for the BBC in October '67, after being used as the B-side of 'Flaming' in the US.

CHAPTER 24
(BARRETT)

Both lyrics and title are derived from the I Ching, a 5,000 year old Chinese book of prophecies – a kind of horoscope, based on randomly-thrown coins rather than astrological coincidences. The lyrics, recited over a fairly simple keyboard drone with a few lightly tickled cymbals, are virtually a rewrite of a chapter (the twenty-fourth!) which suggests new beginnings.

SCARECROW
(BARRETT)

As well as being the B-side to 'See Emily Play' (the only one of the early single sides to appear on an album, compilations aside) 'Scarecrow', another nursery song, was part of the first '67 BBC session.

BIKE
(BARRETT)

Although it seems to be yet another of Barrett's charming and childlike ditties, 'Bike' has a deeper significance. First, there is the very adult plea to Barrett's "girl", then the coda, a manic representation of a "room full of musical tunes", reached by footsteps like those later used to startling effect on the band's quadrophonic PA, the winding of clockwork mechanisms and finally the hauntingly oppressive chattering voices.

At one time planned to segue with 'Interstellar Overdrive', 'Bike' later closed the 'Relics' compilation.

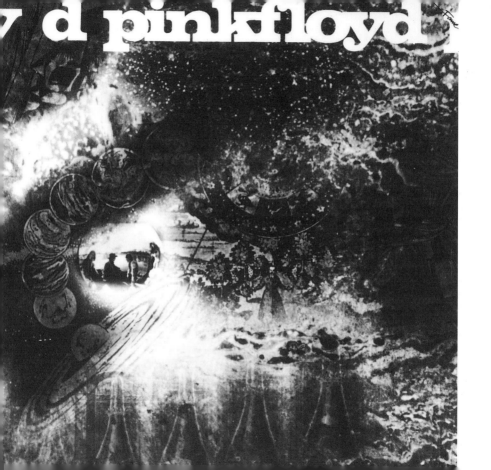

a saucerful of secrets

EMI 8 29751 2; originally Columbia SCX 6258; first issued on CD as EMI CDP 7 46383 2, released June 29 1968

UK Chart: No 9; US Chart: n/a

During the recording of 'Saucerful...', the one secret the band had been trying to keep from their public – the fragile state of Syd Barrett's mental health and his impending breakdown – became uncontainable. It was originally announced that his school friend and one time fellow busker David Gilmour would replace him for live work, with Barrett retaining responsibility for writing, but only a handful of gigs were performed as a five piece and out Barrett went. One result of these changes was an album, again produced by Norman Smith, recorded under great stress by two different line ups. Some tracks were recorded more than once, first with Barrett and then with Gilmour. Mystery has always surrounded some of these sessions, and it is thought that Barrett and Gilmour may be heard together on some tracks – after all, Gilmour was hired partly for his ability to sound like Barrett, whom he had taught to play. During the later sessions, Barrett would sit patiently in the reception area at Abbey Road, waiting to be asked to play for "his" band.

The sleeve was by Storm Thorgerson (formerly a class-mate of Waters and friend of Barrett) and Aubrey 'Po' Powell, working as Hipgnosis, and was the first on which an EMI act, other than The Beatles, had been allowed to use an outside design team. A collage of mystical images, it has none of the panache of their later work.

Again, the mono version of the original vinyl album (Columbia SC 6258) featured different mixes, although less noticeably so than on its predecessor. 'Saucerful...' later formed the second part of the 'A Nice Pair' vinyl reissue, alongside 'Piper...'

Although the 'Saucerful...' sessions began and ended at Abbey Road, some took place at Sound Techniques and De Lane Lea. These also resulted in 'Apples and Oranges' and 'Paintbox', which would end up as either side of the third single, and two tracks, 'Scream Thy Last Scream' and 'Vegetable Man', which, although widely bootlegged and recorded for the October '67 BBC session, remain unreleased, much to the dismay of fans. All four are Syd Barrett compositions and feature his singing and playing.

LET THERE BE MORE LIGHT
(WATERS)

This simple tale of a "close encounter of the third kind" spends its first minute demonstrating the powers of stereophonic imagery. The idea of the band as science fiction fanatics – "space rockers", indeed – was to be a millstone round their collective neck for some time, causing them much irritation.

Vocal duties fell to Gilmour and Wright – an early indication that, for the next 15 years at least, Pink Floyd's three vocalists would be used where their voices fitted best, regardless of who had written the song in question.

This was one of the numbers recorded for the band's first BBC Session with Gilmour, in August 1968. The few live performances include one for *Tous En Scène*.

REMEMBER A DAY
(WRIGHT)

This charming reminiscence of the simplicity of childhood is an out-take from 'Piper...', where some say it was to go under the title 'Sunshine', although there is also evidence to suggest that 'Sunshine' may have been an early version of 'Matilda Mother'. In any case, Syd Barrett plays guitar, although recording was finished after his departure and the vocals are by its composer. It was later included on 'Relics'.

SET THE CONTROLS FOR THE HEART OF THE SUN
(WATERS)

Pink Floyd performed this simple, hypnotic mantra, whose title is a quote from William S. Burroughs, for their first BBC session in

October '67, obviously with Syd on guitar. He is known to have been involved in recording an early version for 'Saucerful...', although David Gilmour also recalls being asked to overdub some guitar, so it is possible that this is the only recording by the five-man Floyd. This is far from certain, as the take with Syd may not be the one released. Waters claimed to have found the lyrics in a book of translated Chinese poetry.

Live versions can be found on 'Ummagumma', the Dutch video *Stamping Ground*, filmed at the Kralingen Pop Festival, of June 1970, and on *Live At Pompeii*. Pink

Floyd performed lengthy renditions until the end of 1973 and eleven years later it was revamped by Roger Waters for his 'Pros And Cons...'tour.

CORPORAL CLEGG
(WATERS)

Syd, by his own admission, does not play on this early indication of Waters' scorn for the military, a theme which would become familiar to followers of the band over the next two and a half decades. The suffering war veteran of the title may have been inspired by the hero of a 1962 Hammer Horror film, *Night Creatures*, one Captain Clegg. The kazoo solo is probably unique in the annals of popular music history. For which we should be thankful.

A SAUCERFUL OF SECRETS
(WATERS/WRIGHT/MASON/GILMOUR)

At the end of the recording sessions, with Syd already well out of the picture, the band's reward for compromising and recording some short pop songs was to be allowed to put down something more representative of their live show. The result was a twenty minute instrumental, divided into four sections,

although these were not given titles until the live version was released on 'Ummagumma' in 1969 – and even later copies of that album omitted to mention them. With no clear indication of where the composers considered the subdivisions to be, the following times are at best a rough guide only.

The first part, 'Something Else', derived from a recording of a very closely miked cymbal, describes, according to David Gilmour, preparations for war. 'Syncopated Pandemonium' (3'59") is a Mason drum pattern, recorded to tape then cut and re-spliced, over which Gilmour abuses his guitar with a microphone stand, and represents the battle itself. There is a cross-fade into 'Storm Signal' (7'02"), with more keyboard generated noises, which is the aftermath. Finally, 'Celestial Voices' (8'39"), all sweeping organ and dreamy vocalese, which one can honestly say is quite beautiful, is thus the requiem.

The structure of the piece was determined by Mason and Waters – both former architecture students – who drew a series of peaks and troughs on a chart to outline its dynamics. The track paved the way for other, perhaps more structured, pieces that would evolve, via

'Atom Heart Mother' and 'Echoes', into 'The Dark Side Of The Moon'.

Until corrected on the remastered CD, David Gilmour's first professional songwriting credit was misspelled 'Gilmore'.

First performed under the title "The Massed Gadgets of Hercules" for a BBC session in June '68, recorded for 'Ummagumma' and later seen in the *Stamping Ground* video, the 'Saucerful...' suite remained in the live set until September 1972, when it was put to rest after being filmed for *Live At Pompeii.*

SEE SAW
(WRIGHT)

Another Wright song on which Syd Barrett is believed to play, its apt working title of 'The Most Boring Song I've Ever Heard Bar Two', begs the question "what on earth were the other two?".

JUGBAND BLUES
(BARRETT)

The only Barrett composition, and his only vocal performance, to make it onto the second album was originally intended, at least by Peter Jenner and Andrew King, as the follow-up to the band's second single, 'See Emily Play'.

The song isn't a blues, nor is it performed by a jug-band (a forerunner of skiffle groups), although Barrett did bring members of a Salvation Army band into De Lane Lea studios to contribute to the chaotic middle section. Quite what these upright Bible-bashers made of being told to "play what you like" is probably best not thought about, but the result makes a chilling accompaniment to Barrett's schizophrenic lyrics, giving the album a very down-beat ending indeed, especially the haunting vocals after the false ending.

For the version recorded for their BBC session on the last day of December '67, the band were without the "assistance" of William Booth's finest and had to create their own discordant middle section.

This is the only track with notable differences between the stereo and mono versions, the latter having more guitar and different vocals. In Canada, 'A Nice Pair' included a different stereo mix, unknown elsewhere.

soundtrack from the film

MORE

pink floyd

played and composed by the

more

**EMI CDP 7 46386 2; originally Columbia SCX 6346,
released: 27 July 1969**

UK Chart: No. 9; US Chart: No. 153

It is a measure of the reputation that Pink Floyd were building for themselves that they were asked to provide a film soundtrack so early in their career, and that they were able to produce it themselves at a time when record companies generally appointed house producers, who would often treat bands as junior employees, to work with them.

Quite what the freaks from the underground, who probably didn't notice Gilmour step into Barrett's shoes on 'Piper...', made of such a marked change in direction so early in the life of the band, no one knows, but the change was as great as any made in the rest of their career.

The 'More' sleeve has a simple, solarised still from the film, "designed" by Hipgnosis. The full wording on the sleeve reads "Soundtrack from the film MORE played and composed by *The* Pink Floyd", using the definite article which was to prove hard for the band to shake off for the next quarter of a century.

Pink Floyd spent just eight days putting music to a plot centred around drug-taking hippies in Ibiza, although some of the songs had made their live débuts sometime earlier. The film was not a success, and has only briefly been available on video, except in France, where it is held in similar regard to *Easy Rider* (the dialogue is all in French) and can still be obtained in SECAM format, incompatible with most other countries' video systems. Without having seen the film, which was directed by Barbet Schroeder, it's difficult to know where the music fits, although some of the titles indicate the sort of mood the tracks were obviously intended to create.

As was often the case, the music heard in the cinema is very different from that re-recorded for the album. In particular, the song 'Seabirds', heard as background music during a party scene, did not make it onto record. It did feature in *The Pink Floyd Songbook* (Lupus Music/ Music Sales, 1976), enabling the only known cover version, by Langford and Kerr, to appear on the 'Moving Soundtracks Vol 1' compilation (Disques Du Crepuscule TWI 122-2).

CIRRUS MINOR
(WATERS)

Named after a type of cloud formation, this opens with a library recording of bird song, descriptively labelled "Dawn Chorus", followed by Rick Wright's over-dubbed Hammond and Farfisa organ tracks and a few gentle vocal lines from David Gilmour.

The recording of this song was featured in a BBC Radio Three documentary *Laying Down Tracks*.

THE NILE SONG
(WATERS)

In which Pink Floyd go heavy metal, Gilmour's shouted vocals contrasting starkly with those in the preceding number. Its strength impressed sufficiently to warrant release as a single in Europe (but not the UK), Japan and New Zealand.

CRYING SONG
(WATERS)

The album switches back to lullaby mode just as quickly, adding a laid-back, jazzy feel courtesy of Waters' mellow bass riff.

The lyric "Help me roll away the stone" is Waters' first use of an image that would resurface on 'Animals' and 'The Wall'.

UP THE KHYBER
(MASON/WRIGHT)

The only writing collaboration by its authors in the band's history is a two minute instrumental, with Mason's hypnotic drumming complemented by Wright's avant-garde piano stabs, and choppy organ riffs.

The title, worthy of the "Carry On" team at their most risqué, refers to the hippies' associations with The Khyber Pass, which links Pakistan with Afghanistan, and has been the scene of both mystic aspirations and military tension for many years, being the route used by many invaders of (what was once) India, including Persians, Greeks, Tartars, Mughals, Alexander The Great and the British, who turned it into a key border post during the occupation of India.

GREEN IS THE COLOUR
(WATERS)

A blend of tin whistle, upright piano and Gilmour's almost whispered vocals give this lyrically-obscure song a charming, folksy feel.

Used as the first part of 'The Journey', imaginatively titled 'The Beginning', it was segued into 'Careful With That Axe, Eugene'. This pairing was recorded for the band's last studio session for BBC Radio One, in May 1969, some time before the sessions for the film soundtrack, performed for the 1970 *In Concert* broadcast and remained together in the live set until dropped in mid- '71, to make way for 'Echoes'.

CYMBALINE
(WATERS)

With lyrics such as "will the final couplet rhyme?" (it doesn't!) and "your manager and agent are both busy on the phone/ selling colour photographs to magazines back home", Waters was obviously beginning to feel the pressures inherent in the industry of which he was forced to be part in order to carry out his craft. The theme would be repeated many, many times throughout his career, and was further evidenced by the song's title when it was performed as part of 'The Man' – 'Nightmare'.

The title may be borrowed from Shakespeare's play *Cymbeline*, although why this should be so is not apparent. Wright produces another of his "Turkish Delight" organ solos and, although Waters handled the lyrics for the version heard in the film, Gilmour sings a slightly rewritten version of them for the album.

Another feature of the May 1969 BBC session, 'Cymbaline' became something of a live favourite, the band often performing very lengthy versions until it was demoted from the set-list at the end of 1971.

PARTY SEQUENCE
(WATERS/WRIGHT/GILMOUR/MASON)

This one-minute instrumental, consisting of some vaguely Arabic-sounding reed instrument, played over Mason's frantic drum pattern, has the distinction of being the shortest studio recording in the Pink Floyd cannon.

MAIN THEME
(WATERS/WRIGHT/GILMOUR/MASON)

The introductory cymbal-tickling is as likely to be Waters' work as Mason's, as it was one of his favourite on-stage pastimes at that time. Soon the track settles into one of his trademark repetitive bass riffs, over which Wright's organ, Mason's drums, a small dose of guitar and synthesiser washes discreetly mingle. Briefly included in the live set during 1970, the tune was extended to fourteen minutes on one memorable occasion. Mason is denied his credit on the CD issue.

IBIZA BAR
(WATERS/WRIGHT/GILMOUR/MASON)

Same tune as 'The Nile Song', performed in a slightly (but only just) lighter mood.

MORE BLUES
(WATERS/WRIGHT/GILMOUR/MASON)

This really is a blues, suggesting, whatever the credit, that Gilmour played a key part in its composition.

QUICKSILVER
(WATERS/WRIGHT/GILMOUR/MASON)

A shimmering instrumental which also formed the basis of 'Sleeping', part of 'The Man'. Some of the electronic sounds used are reminiscent of 'On The Run' from 'Dark Side...'..

A SPANISH PIECE
(GILMOUR)

In the film, this was heard coming from a radio in a bar. The cod-Spanish spoken parts (sounding like Fawlty Towers' Manuel on a bad trip) are, in reality, Pink Floyd's David Gilmour having a bad idea.

DRAMATIC THEME
(WATERS/WRIGHT/GILMOUR/MASON)

Another short instrumental, incorrectly credited to just Waters and Wright on the CD version, with Gilmour's guitar beginning to soar as his inimitable style made its first, tentative appearance on record.

the massed gadgets of auximines

(Live performances only)

At this point in the Pink Floyd story, it would be useful to clarify a phenomenon of their 1969 concerts. Under the generic title 'The Massed Gadgets Of Auximines', they performed two suites, 'The Man' and 'The Journey', each roughly the length of an album side and comprising a number of pieces, some of which were more familiar under other names, some of which were new, and which were never recorded in their own right. Although the idea of recording them as an album was abandoned because so much of the material was borrowed from earlier records, these suites can clearly be seen as the forerunners of 'Atom Heart Mother', 'Echoes' and 'The Dark Side Of The Moon'. Composer credits for some of the numbers can be deduced by reference to their album equivalents.

'The Man' was made up of:

DAYBREAK

A band performance of 'Grantchester Meadows'.

WORK

During the piece, according to a bootlegged Dutch radio broadcast, the band performed a little carpentry on stage. A very jazzy tune, it also featured a trombone solo, almost certainly played by Rick Wright, and Gilmour's very "heavy metal" guitar solo. The studio version, 'Biding My Time', has only ever been released on 'Relics'.

AFTERNOON

A break for the band, with roadies serving tea on stage. Roger Waters repeated this exercise on the Radio KAOS tour.

DOING IT!

A short drum solo.

SLEEPING

A predominantly keyboard instrumental, similar to 'Quicksilver'. During its introduction, a tape of breathing sounds, the band members apparently "slept" on stage.

NIGHTMARE

'Cymbaline'.

DAYBREAK

An instrumental reprise.

'The Journey' was made up of:

THE BEGINNING

'Green Is The Colour', which segued into...

BESET BY CREATURES OF THE DEEP

'Careful With That Axe, Eugene'.

THE NARROW WAY

A band version of what was to become Part 3 of David Gilmour's solo contribution to 'Ummagumma'.

THE PINK JUNGLE

'Pow R. Toc H.'

THE LABYRINTHS OF AUXIMINES

An instrumental, based on the middle section of 'Interstellar Overdrive'.

BEHOLD THE TEMPLE OF LIGHT

Another instrumental.

THE END OF THE BEGINNING

The 'Celestial Voices' part of 'A Saucerful Of Secrets'.

PINK FLOYD

EMI
AEMIST

ummagumma

EMI 8 31202 2; originally Harvest SHDW 1/2; first issued on CD as EMI CDS 7 46404 8, released October 25 1969

UK Chart: No. 5; US Chart: No. 74

Released just three months after 'More', 'Ummagumma' took its unlikely name from a slang word for sex. Pink Floyd had moved sideways from one EMI subsidiary label to another, new, one, Harvest, intended by its founder Malcolm Jones to capture the spirit of the new, progressive underground music. Harvest took the brave step of allowing the band to combine a straightforward live album with a second disc, comprising four sections, each recorded by one band member as a solo activity, guided, for the last time, by a bemused Norman Smith. This was Harvest's first ever double album, and the first record on the label to chart. The studio sessions coincided with those for Syd Barrett's first solo album 'The Madcap Laughs', which Gilmour and Waters partly produced.

The live sides, produced by the band, were recorded at two concerts, the first at Birmingham's legendary Mothers Club on 27 April 1969, the other on 2 May at the Chamber of Commerce, Manchester. Radio One DJ John Peel, at whose wedding Nick Mason was best man, once described the burglary of his flat, where the only item stolen was an acetate copy of a recording of 'Interstellar Overdrive', then under consideration for inclusion on the album.

Aside from 'Grantchester Meadows', and perhaps the final part of 'The Narrow Way', the solo sides are a brave experiment that fails, or at least has dated badly, and although the various pieces are interesting on first hearing, they certainly don't bear repeated listening. All in all, it's a shame that Pink Floyd didn't opt for a more conventional double live album, perhaps recording 'The Man' and 'The Journey' in their entirety.

Hipgnosis' intriguing design for the album included the sleeve of the cast recording of the musical *Gigi*, which was subsequently airbrushed from US versions – perhaps because of copyright problems. The rear sleeve depicted the band's roadies (one of whom is Alan Stiles, later immortalised in 'Alan's Psychedelic Breakfast') and equipment, spread-eagled on a runway at Biggin Hill airfield. Inside the gatefold sleeve, Roger Waters was pictured with his first wife Jude. For the first CD booklet, she was discreetly omitted, as was the Biggin Hill shot.

It has been suggested that the subdivision of three of the solo contributions and 'Saucerful...' may have more to do with ensuring the fair division of royalties than purely musical considerations.

The first track recorded for the album, and never completed, was a group composition, 'Embryo'. The band were horrified when it was included on a compilation of Harvest material, 'Picnic' (Harvest SHSS 1/2), which they insisted be withdrawn immediately. Despite this, 'Embryo' was performed live on many occasions up until the end of 1971, having first appeared in the BBC session recorded in December '68, and can still be obtained on the 'Works' compilation CD in the US.

The remastered UMMAGUMMA was the most radical of the 1994 repackaging exercises, being presented as two separate discs (Live: 8 31213 2; Studio: 8 31214 2) in an embossed card slipcase, with a fold-out poster of the album cover. The Biggin Hill shot was resurrected, and joined by several new shots from that session, but the individual band portraits were all different to the originals. Jude remained absent and the new in-concert shots dated from 1974 or after. The studio disc listed the lyrics for 'Grantchester Meadows', but not 'The Narrow Way Part 3'

ASTRONOMY DOMINE
(BARRETT)

Gilmour proved himself perfectly capable of stepping into Barrett's shoes, even on one of the latter's trademark pieces, just as he would do again in 1994. A short organ solo is the only noticeable variation from the original.

CAREFUL WITH THAT AXE, EUGENE
(WATERS/WRIGHT/GILMOUR/MASON)

A splendid rendition of a concert favourite which had previously only been available to record buyers as the B-side to Pink Floyd's fifth (and, until 1979, last) single, 'Point Me At The Sky'. Always better live than on record, Waters' scream could be as chilling as anything ever heard in a Hammer Horror film.

SET THE CONTROLS FOR THE HEART OF THE SUN
(WATERS)

Although almost double the length, this is not dissimilar to the original version on 'Saucerful...', the extra time being accounted for merely by a slower tempo, a meandering middle section of no great merit, and more of Wright's "Turkish Delight" organ.

A SAUCERFUL OF SECRETS
(WATERS/WRIGHT/MASON/GILMOUR)

Labels on original copies of 'Ummagumma', at least in the USA, gave four subdivisions: Something Else; Syncopated Pandemonium; Storm Signal and Celestial Voices, although these titles are omitted from later vinyl pressings and the CD release. They are explained in more detail under the studio version's entry.

SYSYPHUS (PARTS 1-4)
(WRIGHT)

Rick Wright's instrumental contribution to the second half of the album was named after a character in Greek mythology, more usually spelt "Sisyphus", the King who built Corinth and was condemned, in Hades, the underworld, to forever roll a huge stone ball up a hill, only for it to roll back down again (a feeling not unlike trying to unravel Pink Floyd's early history). His crime was to trap Thanatos, the god of death, thereby evading his own end and meaning that no-one else could die.

Part 1 is mystical synthesiser with timpani, while, in places, Part 2 could easily be taken for a romantic-era classical piano sonata, although this image is soon dissipated by Wright's deliberate use of atonal keyboard runs. Part 3 is very experimental, but has little else to recommend it, and Part 4, opening with bird-song, relies heavily on Wright's Mellotron, eventually returning to the theme of Part 1.

Very few audiences were treated to hearing 'Sysyphus' live, though it was included at a notable gig at Birmingham Town Hall in February 1970, when the band were forced to perform an ad-hoc set after the non-arrival of a truck load of equipment.

GRANTCHESTER MEADOWS
(WATERS)

Opening with yet more bird song, the first of Waters' two contributions is a simple song about the beautiful, unspoilt area of Cambridge where he, and other future Floyds, frolicked in their youth (Gilmour was keen on swimming in the nearby River Cam). His tale of larks, foxes and kingfishers captures the essence of the English countryside in summer perfectly. The song segues into the next piece with a fly buzzing between speakers, Waters finally dispatching it with what one assumes is a rolled up copy of an uncomplimentary review.

A band version was performed as 'Daybreak', part of 'The Man', Wright's organ playing being particularly prominent. As 'Daybreak', it was recorded for the May '69 BBC session, using piano instead of organ.

SEVERAL SPECIES OF SMALL FURRY ANIMALS GATHERED TOGETHER IN A CAVE AND GROOVING WITH A PICT
(WATERS)

Waters' other contribution, later parodied in 'To Roger Waters Wherever You Are', by Ron Geesin on his 'As He Stands' album, is a different matter entirely, comprising a variety of tape loops played at different speed and in different directions. In the days of LP records, it was possible, by destroying one's copy, and stylus, to discern such oddities as Waters repeating "Bring back my guitar", saying "That was pretty avant-garde, wasn't it", drumming his hands on a table and ending with an almost inaudible "Thank you" in the left-hand channel. At the right speed, he is heard ranting bad poetry, improvised on the spot, in an even worse Scottish accent. Sadly, one of the few disadvantages of Compact Discs is that the joys of this kind of vinyl abuse are lost to a new generation of Floyd followers. Contrary to oft-repeated rumours, Geesin played no part in the track.

Fortunately for concert goers, the track was never heard live, although Waters' "ranting Scotsman" did surface occasionally during extended performances of 'Embryo'.

THE NARROW WAY
(PARTS 1-3)
(GILMOUR)

Parts 1 and 2 are both instrumental, the former being acoustic guitar with over-dubbed glissandos and high-pitched notes on an electric, the second a much heavier mêlée of electronically treated guitars which segue, via a sustained Moog note, into the third part, a rather pleasant song on which Gilmour was able to demonstrate his talent as a drummer.

Gilmour found great difficulty in writing the lyrics and requested help from Waters, which was refused. His problems were, perhaps, a portent of the dilemma he would find himself in once he assumed leadership of the band.

Part 1 was performed as 'Baby Blue Shuffle in D Major' during the December '68 BBC Session and Part 3, under its own name, as part of 'The Journey', a band effort which in turn was recorded for the BBC in May '69.

THE GRAND VIZIER'S GARDEN PARTY (PART 1 ENTRANCE; PART 2 ENTERTAINMENT; PART 3 EXIT)
(MASON)

It is probable that Mason cheated for Parts One and Three, calling on his then-wife Lindy to play the same short flute tune for both. Lindy was an accomplished flautist, for whom Ron Geesin wrote music.

Part 2 is a series of percussion exercises, some treated electronically, and which, like the majority of solo drum recordings, go on far, far too long, but not as long as the Turkish Empire, where The Grand Vizier was a senior official.

zabriskie point

EMI CDP 7 94217 2; originally MGM 2315 002,
released March 1970

Pink Floyd's third major soundtrack project, for Michelangelo Antonioni, didn't go as well as the first two. After two weeks in the studio, much of their work was rejected for being "Too sad" or "Too strong". Eventually, Antonioni substituted tracks by The Grateful Dead and such legendary superstars as Roscoe Holcomb and John Fahey. He did use four cuts, and several out-takes from the sessions are available on bootlegs, although the titles by which the latter have become known, 'Oneone', 'Fingal's Cave' and 'Rain In The Country', may be the inventions of bootleggers, rather than the band themselves. Another piece, 'The Violent Sequence', intended to accompany a scene depicting riots at the University of California in Los Angeles, with emphasis on the brutality of the police, would resurface on 'Dark Side...'.

Of course, the music in the film is different to what we hear on record, including an untitled instrumental, lasting about one minute, which isn't on the album at all. The film is not available on video in the UK.

HEAT BEAT, PIG MEAT
(WATERS/GILMOUR/MASON/WRIGHT)

An organ and drums based instrumental, written for the opening credits. Some dialogue is heard on the released version, as is a snatch of classical string music.

CRUMBLING LAND
(WATERS/GILMOUR/MASON/WRIGHT)

This is longer than the version heard in the film, but an even longer take has been bootlegged. The vocals, shared by Gilmour and Wright, seem to relate to the plot of the film.

COME IN NO. 51, YOUR TIME IS UP
(WATERS/GILMOUR/MASON/WRIGHT)

Yet another remake of 'Careful With That Axe, Eugene', this is used at the end of the film, to accompany slow-motion images of a building exploding. The scream is one of Waters' best.

atom heart mother

**EMI 8 31246 2; originally Harvest SHVL 781;
first issued on CD as EMI CDP 7 46381 2,
released: October 10 1970**

UK Chart: No. 1; US Chart: No. 55

Produced by "The" Pink Floyd (that troublesome definitive article again, dropped for the CD booklets), at Abbey Road, with Alan Parsons credited as one of the studio engineers and Norman Smith "promoted" to executive producer, 'Atom Heart Mother' was the Harvest label's first British Number one. It is difficult to imagine such a radical piece of music topping the charts these days, or indeed ever again.

'Atom Heart Mother' was the first Pink Floyd album to be released (as Harvest Q4SHVL 781) for the new Quadrophonic, or four-speaker system; a particularly appropriate move, since they had been using quadrophonic, and even six-way, sound in their concerts since 1969. Indeed, they still use a four-way split to this day.

The cover is now better known than the music within, starring a bemused looking, and deliberately bemusing, cow (Lulubelle III, if you must know), photographed by Hipgnosis with the specific intention of having a cover which had no meaning, and was not related in any way to the music. Further cow photographs were added to the 1994 reissue, which also offers much crisper sound.

ATOM HEART MOTHER (FATHER'S SHOUT; BREAST MILKY; MOTHER FORE; FUNKY DUNG; MIND YOUR THROATS PLEASE; REMERGENCE)

(MASON/GILMOUR/WATERS/WRIGHT/GEESIN)

The album's side-long title track was orchestrated and co-composed by Ron Geesin, with whom Waters had already recorded a film soundtrack, 'The Body'. He was handed rough tapes by the band who, with only a few pointers, asked him to overdub "something grand". Geesin used the cello player from 'The Body', ten brass players and twenty-strong choir. When the politics of working with so many session players (classical musicians are notoriously difficult in such circumstances) proved too much for him, choir leader John Aldiss took over from Geesin as conductor. Geesin still considers the released version to be little better than a demo and wanted at the time to re-record the piece. As, indeed, did the band, but time and funds forbade such a luxury.

At its début performance, in Paris in February 1970, Roger Waters introduced the suite as 'The Amazing Pudding'. It did not gain its familiar title until it was performed, in September 1970, at the BBC's Paris Theatre, for an *In Concert* broadcast. Asked for a title for the programme's log sheet, so the story goes, the band hurriedly scanned a newspaper, eventually borrowing the headline from a story about a woman with an "atom powered" (sic) pacemaker.

Further live performances followed, both with and without an accompanying orchestra and choir, lasting anything from fourteen to thirty minutes, including the première of the "orchestral" version at the Bath festival, which Ron Geesin left mid-performance. Others were more impressed, and the piece led to Pink Floyd being the first and only rock band to perform at the prestigious Montreux festival of classical music.

For the curious, the various parts begin at 5'19", 10'09", 15'25", 17'44" and 19'45", although they are not indexed individually on the 1994 CD, as they were on the first version, at least for listeners with equipment capable of reading such subdivisions.

IF
(WATERS)

The deceptive simplicity of the opening lines and uncomplicated, acoustic guitar do not prepare the listener for the sudden switch to references to insanity and loneliness. It was an early sign to those in the know that Syd's influence – or, more specifically, guilt over his departure – would stay with Waters for a while yet.

Although the band never performed 'If' live (except as part of the above-mentioned BBC *In Concert* show), it was released as a single in the US and mainland Europe. In the Eighties, Roger Waters revived it for his Pros & Cons and Radio KAOS tours.

SUMMER '68
(WRIGHT)

Although Wright claims never to have been happy as a lyric writer, he does concede that this song, questioning a casual pick-up or possibly a groupie, embodies his own true feelings. Even so, it is the only track on the album never to have been played live.

The "brass" interlude is played on an early synthesiser, with Wright singing the verses and Gilmour the heavier choruses.

FAT OLD SUN
(GILMOUR)

Gilmour wrote this very English song as a sequel to 'Grantchester Meadows'. From the opening church bells to the gentle acoustic guitar and muted drums, it is a perfect vehicle for the most mellow singing of his career. It was recorded for two BBC *In Concert* shows, the 1970 one referred to already, and one in October 1971, as well as becoming a regular part of the '70 and '71 live sets.

ALAN'S PSYCHEDELIC BREAKFAST (RISE AND SHINE; SUNNY SIDE UP; MORNING GLORY)
(WATERS/MASON/GILMOUR/WRIGHT)

Thirteen minutes of tomfoolery, named after a Pink Floyd roadie Alan Stiles, whose voice can be heard as he performs his morning ritual. One of its keyboard riffs would later reappear as the basis of 'Profiles', the title track of Nick Mason's second solo album.

Between musical passages, Stiles is heard

ATOM HEART MOTHER : PINK FLOYD

washing himself and frying bacon. Such *musique concrète*, or non-musical sound, was to become a hallmark of almost every Pink Floyd album, but none would use it as much as this piece, which was performed live, unsurprisingly, only once, at Sheffield City Hall in December 1970. During the performance, the band brewed tea and cooked on stage.

The dripping tap which closes the piece originally continued, *ad infinitum*, in the album's run-out groove. The track's subdivisions are at 4'29" and 8'18".

relics

Music For Pleasure MFP 50397 (not on CD); originally Starline
SRS 5071, released: May 14 1971

UK Chart: No. 32; US Chart: No. 152

Tracks: Arnold Layne; Interstellar Overdrive; See Emily Play; Remember A Day;
Paintbox; Julia Dream; Careful With That Axe, Eugene; Cirrus Minor; The Nile Song;
Biding My Time; Bike.
Following the chart success of 'Atom Heart Mother', EMI's budget subsidiary Starline
released this compilation of early singles, album tracks and the otherwise unreleased
Waters composition 'Biding My Time', only ever played live as 'Work' in 'The Man' suite.

The sleeve is graced by Nick Mason's pen and ink drawing – shaded pink on later releases – with its subtitle, 'A Bizarre Collection of Antiques and Curios'. Overseas, two alternative covers have been used. Australia's showed old Spanish coins, while in America a grotesque bottle opener, fashioned to represent a head with two pairs of eyes, was depicted. The Japanese version had a gatefold sleeve with Mason's drawing.

EMI Australia briefly released RELICS on CD (EMI CDAX 701290). This occurred without the band's consent, hence its rapid withdrawal.

At the time of writing, EMI are considering a CD version, possibly with a revised tracklisting.

meddle

**EMI 8 29749 2; originally Harvest SHVL 795;
first issued on CD as Harvest CDP 7 46034 2,
released: November 13 1971**

UK Chart: No. 3; US Chart: No. 70

Regarded by many as the album where the band first showed its mettle – no doubt a reflection of David Gilmour's growing confidence – 'Meddle' comprises two tone poems and four fairly standard songs, produced by the band at Air Studios (the band's first 16 track sessions), Abbey Road, Morgan Sound and Wright's kitchen. Work was said to have been done on a quadrophonic mix, but if this exists, it has never seen the light of day.

The sleeve is another Hipgnosis creation: a pig's ear, under rippling water, representing the echoes of the lead track – ideal for a band for whom sonic qualities have often been as important as tunes and words.

ONE OF THESE DAYS
(MASON/GILMOUR/WATERS/WRIGHT)

In the *Live At Pompeii* film – and often at concerts – this was referred to by its full, somewhat unfriendly title, 'One Of These Days, I'm Going To Cut You Into Little Pieces', as declaimed by Nick Mason's solitary, slowed down, vocal contribution.

The opening wind gives way to a menacing bass riff (courtesy of a device called a Binson echo unit) which itself precedes staccato keyboards and solid, if unadventurous drumming, before some convincing slide guitar. The bass guitar is double tracked, with Gilmour playing on one stereo channel and Waters following on the other. The naggingly familiar tune just after the three minute mark is a light-hearted snatch of the theme to television favourite *Doctor Who*.

Always a live favourite, it was included in the BBC *In Concert* show of October 1971, the last time they performed specifically for the BBC (the recording also included a blues instrumental, which has only ever been broadcast in the US). It opened the second set on the 1987-88 tour, while nightly performances in 1994 yielded a live version for the B-side of the 'High Hopes'/'Keep Talking' single.

In *Live At Pompeii*, Gilmour plays the piece on his usual Stratocaster, but for more recent live performances, he has preferred a pedal steel guitar, as can clearly be seen in the *Delicate Sound Of Thunder* video.

A PILLOW OF WINDS
(GILMOUR/WATERS)

More pastoral, dreamy Englishness, held together by Rick Wright's organ, despite its low place in the mix. Like 'Fearless' and 'San Tropez', this never warranted a live performance, suggesting that they were seen by the band, to some degree, as filler.

FEARLESS
(GILMOUR/WATERS)

Unremarkable, although Waters' lyrics, sung by Gilmour over the latter's tune, hint at things to come. The coda is an *a cappella* rendition of Rodgers & Hammerstein's 'You'll Never Walk Alone' recorded at the Kop end of Liverpool F.C.'s Anfield ground, where it was the crowd's anthem.

SAN TROPEZ
(WATERS)

A jazzy little number with emphasis on Wright's piano. Gilmour's unexpected Hawaiian guitar middle eight is unfamiliar territory, but still manages to demonstrate his virtuosity.

SEAMUS
(MASON/GILMOUR/WATERS/WRIGHT)

A canine throwaway, it's a pity a better vehicle could not have been found for Gilmour's authentic-sounding bluegrass guitar work.

The performance at Pompeii under the bizarre title 'Mademoiselle Nobs', with Gilmour's vocals replaced by his harmonica playing and Waters switching to electric guitar, was to be the track's only live outing – perhaps Wright's dog's rider was too demanding?

ECHOES
(MASON/GILMOUR/WATERS/WRIGHT)

The band filled the second side of the album with a twenty-three and a half minute master-piece, composed by linking together twenty-odd short riffs and themes, in turn the results of studio jamming with tapes running. They were given the working title of 'Nothing, Parts 1-24'. As the work progressed, tapes were labelled, in the style of a Japanese monster movie, 'Son Of Nothing' and 'The Return Of The Son Of Nothing', a mundane explanation of the rather mystical-sounding name some-times given to the track by bootleggers. The lyrics of early performances made reference to planets and space, but by the time of its release, the message had become more inward looking.

The opening "sonar" ping was discovered by accident when Rick fed his piano through a Leslie amplifier. Much time was later expend-ed trying to recapture the exact sound, but when this proved impossible, the effect had to be edited from one of the original demos, recorded at Abbey Road. Other than that, 'Echoes' was recorded entirely at Air Studios.

The tension in the crescendo leading up to the third verse is truly awesome, but the verse itself is no anticlimax, more a post-coital glow. Listening to live tapes, one could sympathise with an audience that never wanted the music to end.

'Echoes' was used to good effect in the film *Pink Floyd – Live At Pompeii* where it was performed, in two parts, book-ending the concert with no audience. It was also the highlight of the band's 1971 BBC *In Concert* recording. Another performance was recorded by the BBC in 1974, at the same time as the 'Dark Side...' *In Concert*. Apparently, it's absolutely wonderful, but the band have always refused to allow it to be broadcast.

The middle passage of 'Echoes' was occasionally borrowed for live performances of 'Embryo'. To best understand how this section was recorded, budding guitar superstars should watch Gilmour's performance in *Live At Pompeii*.

Despite their growing live success, Roger Waters sometimes expressed his boredom during concerts by introducing the piece with silly names. 'Looking Through The Knotholes In Granny's Wooden Leg' was one, as was 'We Won The Double', after his football team, Arsenal, won both the league title and FA Cup in 1971. 'The March Of The Dambusters' might also have been funny, had Pink Floyd not been playing in Germany at the time!

The studio recording of 'Echoes' also featured in a lengthy sequence of the surfing film *Crystal Voyager*, where it accompanies scenes shot by a surfboard-mounted camera with waves breaking all around. This obviously impressed the band, as they used the same images when the track was performed live on the opening handful of dates of Pink Floyd's 1987 tour. Sadly, it was dropped all too soon, the band apparently becoming bored with it. In the early 1990's, an advertising agency attempted to obtain clearance to use 'Echoes' and the Crystal Voyager footage to promote a toilet cleaner. They were unsuccessful.

obscured by clouds

EMI CDP 7 46385 2;
originally Harvest SHSP 4020,
released: June 3 1972

UK Chart: No. 6; US Chart: No. 46

Produced by Pink Floyd in less than two weeks, at the famous Château d'Herouville near Paris, this is the soundtrack to the movie La Vallée (also known as Obscured By Clouds), by *More* director Barbet Schroeder. Like "More", the music on the album is different from the short extracts heard in the film, which is also unavailable on video outside France, perhaps because the dialogue is again in French. It tells the tale of a bunch of hippies (yawn) going native as they search for a lost valley in New Guinea.

The cover shot is a deliberately out of focus still from the film, lacking any of the cleverness one would expect of Hipgnosis.

Very much overlooked by casual fans, of all the band's creations this is justifiably one of Nick Mason's favourites.

OBSCURED BY CLOUDS
(WATERS/GILMOUR)

A pulsing instrumental, whose opening synthesiser riff was blatantly ripped off for an aftershave advert in the Eighties.

WHEN YOU'RE IN
(WATERS/GILMOUR/MASON/WRIGHT)

Very similar to the preceding track, but with more prominent drums, the two being performed as one number throughout 1973.

BURNING BRIDGES
(WRIGHT/WATERS)

Sung by Gilmour and Wright, this otherwise insignificant little ballad is made memorable by neat guitar work, which has very little in common with Gilmour's work on subsequent albums. It is one of only three joint compositions by Wright and Waters, the others being 'Stay' and 'Us And Them'.

THE GOLD IT'S IN THE...
(WATERS/GILMOUR)

This raucous rocker, sung by Gilmour, benefits from the rawness forced on the band by the short deadlines to which they were working, and puts to death the myth that they were nothing without studio trickery.

WOT'S... UH THE DEAL
(WATERS/GILMOUR)

For the first half of this song, Gilmour sings over some simple acoustic guitar, later joined by drums and bass. Wright then contributes a piano solo before Gilmour responds with electric guitar. Despite its lack of Pink Floyd trademarks, the very simplicity of the song makes it

the album's unexpected treasure. But why is there a four-note organ riff in the fade out?

MUDMEN
(WRIGHT/ GILMOUR)

Until 'Cluster One' on 'The Division Bell', this was the only track in Pink Floyd's history on which Wright and Gilmour shared full writing credits. 'Mudmen' is an instrumental vehicle for swirling organ and layers of guitar, including two solos which mark the birth of the style that Gilmour would milk so successfully during the late Seventies and Eighties, both for Floyd albums and during his many guest sessions for other artists.

CHILDHOOD'S END
(GILMOUR)

Other than the contentious first track on 'Dark Side...', this was to be the last song recorded by Pink Floyd without Waters' name attached to it, and Gilmour's last lyric, for the rest of Waters' time with the band. It has been suggested that the title came from the book of the same name by Arthur C. Clarke.

This is very much the composer's track, although his vocals and intense guitar are ably supported by Wright's organ and Mason's drumming, earning it a handful of live performances in late '72 and early '73. The strict-tempo drum pattern laid down by Mason during the second minute would resurface on 'Time'.

FREE FOUR
(WATERS)

Another guitar-starred rocker, taking its title from the ostentatiously enunciated count-in "One, two, 'free, four!" and released as a single in several territories, but not the UK.

The lyrics are Waters' first direct reference to the wartime death of his father, a theme which would be of key importance to 'The Wall' and 'The Final Cut' and, in a more general sense, 'Us And Them' on 'Dark Side...' Waters also manages to include a sideswipe at the Rock'n'Roll circus, bemoaning the need for yet *another* American tour. The latter lyrics were new for the album version, in the film there is a verse very reminiscent of the lines about "taking a slice" in 'Money'. There are other, minor lyrical differences elsewhere in the song.

STAY
(WRIGHT/WATERS)

Sung by Wright, this appears to be a heart-melting love song, a genre not typically associated with Pink Floyd. However, there is a sting in the tail, when in the light of a new morning, the narrator cannot remember the name of the woman he wakes up with (a groupie, perhaps?) and wants her to leave.

ABSOLUTELY CURTAINS
(WATERS/GILMOUR/WRIGHT/MASON)

Perhaps taking advantage of the new studio's facilities, Wright took the opportunity to play not only his usual Mellotron and organ, but something that sounds suspiciously like a harpsichord. The closing two minutes are taken up by the singing of the film's New Guinea natives – Pink Floyd were even ahead of their time with so-called "World Music".

live at pompeii

**4-Front Video 080 730 3;
premièred: September 1972**

Tracks: Instrumental; Echoes Part I; Careful With That Axe, Eugene; A Saucerful Of Secrets; Us and Them; One Of These Days I'm Going To Cut You Into Little Pieces; Set The Controls For The Heart Of The Sun; Brain Damage; Mademoiselle Nobs; Echoes Part II

Another important milestone in the history of Pink Floyd is this film, an audience-free performance shot in the amphitheatre of the Roman town of Pompeii. Despite obvious recourse to studio reworking, the film, directed by Adrian Maben, captures the spirit of the era's live performances superbly. Also included are interviews and scenes of the band at work on 'Dark Side...' in Abbey Road Studios. This includes the memorable David Gilmour quote, after being chided by Roger Waters for allowing an impurity in his guitar sound: "Christ, where would Rock'n'Roll be without feedback" and the less significant Nick Mason utterances about his preference for apple pie *without* crust.

There are two different versions of the opening instrumental, one used in the original film, the other on all the available video versions. Both are insignificant electronic doodles. Be warned that most previous home-video releases of this film have omitted the interviews and Abbey Road footage. The film is also available on Laser Disc.

dark side of the moon

**EMI 8 29752 2; originally Harvest SHVL 804,
released March 1973**

UK Chart: No. 2; US Chart: No. 1

Without a doubt, this is the BIG one. Statistically, it should be playing somewhere or other on the planet during every moment of every day, with a copy in one in five UK households. The record's release was not the suite's début, however, as the very first performance, subtitled 'A Piece For Assorted Lunatics', was in early 1972 and was abruptly halted by a power failure during 'Money'. The title 'Dark Side Of The Moon' is a reference to the occult name for the subconscious. However, Medicine Head released an album of that name in late 1971, so the planned title was changed to "Eclipse". When the Medicine Head album flopped, the original title was revived by the Floyd, but even they weren't sure exactly what to call their new, self produced, album. Original copies prefixed the title as 'The Dark Side...', as did the front of the first CD issue. However, later copies, and both the spine and disc of the first and latest CDs, all omit the troublesome definitive article.

'Dark Side...' was to be the first of a run of albums with all their lyrics by Roger Waters. The importance of his narrative was highlighted by the fact that this was the first Floyd album to have lyrics printed on its sleeve (although the recent CD reissues of earlier albums have had lyrics added retrospectively). The idea of linking songs with themes of madness, ageing, work and death – worries that trouble every one of us – came about in a band meeting in Mason's kitchen.

Recording was done throughout 1972, the

first to take place on Abbey Road's new, 24-track equipment. The album's engineer was Alan Parsons, then paid £35 per week. After receiving an Emmy for his work on the record and going on the road as Pink Floyd's sound mixer, he built an entire career emulating Pink Floyd's sonic soundscapes on his own albums, much to Gilmour's chagrin.

Even at this stage in the band's career, tensions were running high between Waters and Gilmour, and record producer Chris Thomas was brought in to arbitrate between them during the final mixing. This was done in such a way that all the tracks, with the exception of the break between the original vinyl sides, before 'Money', segue into each other. A quad version, Q4SHVL 804, had some subtly different mixes (notably the spoken parts on the final two tracks, as heard on 'Works'), but these were closer to the regular stereo version than other Quad and Mono versions in the Floyd catalogue. However, the quad mix was reissued in Australia on pink vinyl, in 1988. A quad master tape, intended for vinyl pressings, was inadvertently used in the US for the first batch of CDs.

Despite only reaching No. 2 in the UK, and managing only one week at No. 1 in the US, the album's chart performance has never been equalled, and probably never will be. Even taking into account a couple of minor breaks, it has been in the US top 200 for over 800 weeks – over 15 years!

The album's saxophonist was Dick Parry, a relatively unknown session musician, but favoured for sharing his Cambridge roots with the band. He was an inspired choice, and accompanied them on tour for the next two years, and again in 1994.

Apart from Clare Torry's famous contribution (of which more below), backing vocals were performed by well known session singers Liza Strike, Barry St. John and Leslie Duncan, plus veteran gospel performer Doris Troy. A pair of black women singers, Carlena Williams and Vanetta Fields, known as The Blackberries, joined the band for post-album performances of the suite. All in all, the band performed the suite at least 385 times until abandoning it for almost twenty years after the 1975 Knebworth festival. The BBC have a superb performance recorded at Wembley Arena (then the Empire Pool) in 1974, but although this gets an occasional airing, sadly the band have refused requests for it to be granted an official release.

Every track from the album, except 'Speak To Me' and 'Any Colour You Like', has been performed by either Gilmour or Waters on solo tours, and Pink Floyd exhumed the suite for a handful of performances in the USA and Europe in 1994, from which a live release is promised.

The original sleeve is one of the best – and best known – in rock. A triumph of simplicity, it was designed by Hipgnosis and drawn by George Hardie. Hipgnosis offered the band several alternative designs. The meeting, according to Thorgerson, "took about three seconds, in as much as the band cast their eyes over everything, looked at each other, said in unison 'That one' and left the room". The sleeve includes two deliberate mistakes. Firstly, there is no purple in the spectrum, to simplify the design. Secondly, the rear sleeve showed the prism producing a converging spectrum – a physical impossibility, but necessary to allow opened out sleeves to be arranged end-to-end, forming a continuous design, or mandala, useful for in-store displays.

Vinyl copies came with two free stickers and two posters – one a collection of live shots, the other a night view of the pyramids at Giza. For some reason, both are different in American copies, while the Japanese edition came with a lavish booklet. The band had wanted everything to be presented in a box, but EMI vetoed this on the grounds of cost. Twenty years later, they relented and a limited edition boxed CD (EMI 7 81479 2) was released, using a digitally revamped master tape. The box also contained a new booklet, revised artwork and five "art-cards". A year later, the new master was used as one of EMI's series of reissues. Shortly afterwards, the album became the first Pink Floyd minidisc (EMI 8 29752 8).

For all its brighter sound and glossy artwork, the 1994 reissue's packaging is inferior to that of the original album and the first CD. Not only is the comforting familiarity of the airbrushed prism on the front lost to a harsher version taken from a photograph of a real glass prism, but the live and pyramid shots (the original posters were adapted for the first CD's booklet) have been replaced and the photogram backgrounds are just plain tacky.

SPEAK TO ME
(MASON)

Opening with a reassuring heartbeat, this introductory sound collage forms an overture to the rest of the suite, including sounds from the rest of the album, plus the manic laughter and verbal interjections of a road manager (not Pink Floyd's) nicknamed Roger the Hat. His contribution includes the famous "I've been mad for fucking years", which was much more prominent in live performances.

Roger Waters has since claimed that he devised the track and that Mason's credit (his only solo credit outside 'Ummagumma') was merely a gift.

"The Hat"'s contribution, like others heard throughout the album, is from a session where Waters held up cards with questions such as "when did you last thump somebody" or "what do you think of death" on them, recording their responses. One of the participants was Paul McCartney, although his contribution was considered too cautious to be used.

Although listed separately on the latest CD issue, 'Speak To Me' and 'Breathe' are indexed as one track, as they were on the first CD issues. To confuse matters, the CD in the 'Shine On' box set indexes them as two tracks.

BREATHE IN THE AIR
(WATERS/GILMOUR/WRIGHT)

More naming problems occur with this song, which is sometimes listed as just 'Breathe', for example on the remastered CD (the copy in the 'Shine On' box set manages to use both names); perhaps the longer title is intended to distinguish it from another track called 'Breathe', on 'The Body', Waters' 1970 film soundtrack album recorded with Ron Geesin. They share their opening line and, with a little imagination, it is easy to hear how one may have mutated into the other. In contrast, the first line of the second verse is the title of a song which was originally a "hit" in 1939, when Flanagan and Allen sang it in The Crazy Gang's film *The Little Dog Laughed*.

Until using it on the 1994 tour, Pink Floyd only ever performed the track as part of complete 'Dark Side...' shows, but Waters used it as a stand-alone song during the last few concerts of his 1987 tour.

ON THE RUN
GILMOUR/WATERS

The title is Waters' representation of paranoia, a theme reinforced by the concert footage introduced in 1987, with a man strapped to a bed, being wheeled along hospital corridors at ever increasing speeds until it bursts through a pair of doors onto a runway, and takes off. At this point in the concert, an inflatable bed flew down the venue on a wire and exploded in flames on stage. Both music and film have been in the Floyd's live set ever since.

The piece was largely created on a VCS3 synthesiser. Waters is seen piecing together an early version, at Abbey Road, in *Live In Pompeii*, offering a rare insight into the way the band used their studio time. Responsibility for the footsteps in the closing sequence was later claimed by engineer Parsons.

In pre-album concert performances, this part of the suite had been a completely different, guitar-based tune, with a keyboard solo.

TIME
(MASON/WATERS/WRIGHT/GILMOUR)

Famous for its cacophony of chiming clocks,

recorded as a quadrophonic test tape for EMI by Parsons and useful for testing and comparing hi-fi equipment, this indicates Waters' concerns about ageing – remarkable for something written when he was just 28 – and his fear that life was passing him by – ironic for someone about to score such a massive success. Gilmour and Wright, the latter backed by the session singers, take alternate verses, with Wright's being the more mellow style. Gilmour's guitar solo is unequalled, remaining one of his all-time classics. Early live versions were much slower, with some awful harmonies (the term is used loosely!) between Gilmour and Wright.

Waters' lines about "hanging on in quiet desperation" being "the English way", are borrowed from "Walden", the 1854 autobiographical work of American Henry David Thoreau, which reads "The mass of men lead lives of quiet desperation". After the song's final, pessimistic lyric, comes an extra verse, subtitled 'Breathe Reprise', which is missing from a bootlegged alternative take.

A US single release has Mason's opening Rototoms reprised at the end, courtesy of a deft piece of studio editing.

THE GREAT GIG IN THE SKY
(WRIGHT)

This is surely the most seductive song about death ever. At Alan Parsons' suggestion, Clare Torry was brought in to perform the almost painfully beautiful vocalese. She recorded several takes at different volumes and pitches and the track is a compilation of these. Although she improvised her part in the studio, Torry was not given the co-composer's credit that many now feel she deserved, receiving instead double the standard flat fee – a staggering £30!

Torry obviously doesn't hold a grudge, though, as she reprised her performance on stage, both for Roger Waters' London shows in 1987, and with Pink Floyd at Knebworth '90. She later earned a much larger sum when the track became the first Floyd piece to be officially used for a television commercial, in this case for Neurofen painkillers. After seeking permission from Wright (who, as composer, held sole authority to say yea or nay), the agency concerned recruited Torry to re-create the original with session musicians, earning her a repeat fee every time it was screened.

Early live versions, known as 'The Mortality Sequence', were fairly dire, comprising a speech by journalist and moral crusader Malcolm Muggeridge and taped Bible readings, with a keyboard accompaniment. The track returned to Pink Floyd's live set early in 1988, and has remained ever since.

On CD, 'Great Gig' cross-fades into the following track, masking what was originally the break between vinyl sides.

MONEY
(WATERS)

The album's other great piece of *musique concrète* is the speaker-hopping rhythmic till-ringing which heralds its best-known song. This was created by carefully marking the original recording, cutting it into inch-long pieces and painstakingly reassembling it on the studio floor, so that the various tills and coins sounded right on the beat – a task which could have been accomplished in minutes, had the band had access to a modern sampler and sequencer. The aggressive saxophone part was capably handled by Parry.

Waters' reference to Lear Jets is ironic, considering that both Mason and Gilmour went on to qualify as pilots, the latter (who handled the song's vocals) forming a company to own, fly and promote his collection of classic aircraft.

'Money' was released as a single in the US, using an edited version, a rarity only ever released in the UK on the vinyl-only compilation 'Rock Legends' (Telstar STAR 2290). The single's chart success – it reached No. 13 – changed the band's fortunes forever. It also changed their audiences, and they were never again able to play quiet passages without being drowned out by cheerin' and hollerin' fans.

It is the most performed piece in the band's history, used as the encore throughout the 1977 'Animals' tour, played on both Gilmour and Waters' solo tours and at all Pink Floyd's subsequent dates. Gilmour has now performed the track at over 780 concerts!

Waters produced a pseudo-live version for a single B-side in 1987 and Gilmour, when he appeared on Nicky Home's Radio One show in July 1992, allowed the airing of a brief portion of Waters' original demo for the track, with the composer singing to his own crude, double-tracked acoustic guitar accompaniment.

US AND THEM
(WATERS/WRIGHT)

Wright originally composed this tune as a simple piano piece for *Zabriskie Point*, with the descriptive working title of 'The Violent Sequence'. It was given just one pre-'Dark Side...' live airing, at the 1970 gig performed without their usual equipment. It was then 21 minutes long! Wright is seen working on his piano part in the studio segments of *Live At Pompeii*.

This version, unlike the original, is enhanced by Parry's saxophone, in a much more laid-back vein than his strident blowing on 'Money'. Waters sang early live versions, but Gilmour did the honours for the album, with Wright unusually providing the heavier singing on the angrier second and final verses. The anti-war, anti-hierarchy lyrics could have been lifted straight from 'The Wall'.

As well as being an occasional encore on the 1977 tour, 'Us And Them' has been a regular in Pink Floyd's post-Waters concerts.

An early studio version has been bootlegged, with the sax solo mixed very differently.

ANY COLOUR YOU LIKE
(GILMOUR/MASON/WRIGHT)

Believe it or not, this instrumental, a synthesiser and guitar work-out, is the only track in the band's entire canon where the 'other three' wrote together, without Waters, while the latter was still in the band. The title is taken from the oft-misquoted advert for the world's first mass-produced car, the Ford Model T, which offered purchasers the choice of "Any color you like, so long as it's black".

BRAIN DAMAGE
(WATERS)

This, the nearest thing to the album's title track (it is the only song to include the words "the dark side of the Moon"), and the following song, representing Waters' only vocals on the album, have always been performed as a pair, including the encores on the author's '84 and '87 solo outings.

In *Live At Pompeii*, Waters' is seen over-dubbing bass to a tape which already has his completed vocals. Later, Gilmour is seen adding further layers of guitar. A 1972 version is one of the few post-Sixties Pink Floyd out-takes to surface.

The lyric about "the lunatic on the grass" is taken from an unrecorded song Waters wrote during the 'Meddle' sessions in 1971. Its title? 'The Dark Side Of The Moon'!

ECLIPSE
(WATERS)

'Eclipse' demonstrates one of Waters' favourite writing techniques – when in doubt, write a list. This "list-o-mania" can be heard on most of his subsequent albums with Pink Floyd, as well as several of his solo works. The words were not written until, after a few live performances, the band realised that the suite needed some kind of ending.

The album closes with the heartbeat once more, behind which Jerry Driscoll, Abbey Road's doorman, cheerfully adds "There is no dark side of the moon – matter of fact, it's all dark".

Or does it? The pages of *The Amazing Pudding*, the independent Pink Floyd and Roger Waters magazine, were consumed with debate for almost two years in the early Nineties, over a piece of music which could be heard *very* faintly during the final heartbeats. Some claimed it was a figment of readers' warped imaginations, but something resembling a string orchestra playing 'Ticket To Ride' could definitely be heard at the end of Driscoll's line, on the remastered CD, if the volume was set very loud. Other copies, such as the previous UK CD, did not seem to have the same phenomenon, but a whispering voice could be heard at 1'41". Explanations ranged from a Floydian joke to interference during mastering, and from the use of second hand tape to a performance in an adjacent studio being picked up. All seem equally unlikely.

WISH YOU WERE HERE

wish you were here

**EMI 8 29750 2; originally Harvest SHYL 814;
first issued on CD as Harvest CDP 7 46035 2,
released: September 15 1975**

UK Chart: No. 1; US Chart: No. 2

Following 'Dark Side…' was always going to be a problem for the band. Eventually, it took them two years, a great deal of heartache, an abortive experimental album, two (temporarily) abandoned song ideas, the appearance of a high-selling bootleg and the accidental spoiling of a master-tape before they were ready. It was worth the wait. The story does not begin in the studio, however, but with that bootleg.

In 1974 fans began to buy what they believed to be the new Pink Floyd album, 'British Winter Tour '74'. This was, in fact, a well-packaged bootleg, with live recordings of three new songs, 'Raving And Drooling', 'Gotta Be Crazy' and 'Shine On You Crazy Diamond'. Although the latter would be recorded for this album, the other two (which were performed live, in vastly evolved versions, on the 1975 'Wish You Were Here' tour) were not committed to vinyl for another two years, after further changes.

The album was again produced by Pink Floyd, at Abbey Road studios. Although most of the music was composed collaboratively, all the lyrics were by Roger Waters. Tour vocalists Vanetta Fields and Carlena Williams were among the guest musicians joining the band in the studio.

The recording sessions were very difficult

for the band, who had to balance the pressures of success with the fact that they had now achieved all their ambitions. Mason was particularly disinterested, since his marriage (like Waters') was breaking up and drumming came low on his priorities, but the rest of the band were equally affected by boredom, exhaustion and a sense of malaise that made it difficult to concentrate on the minutiae of recording. Indeed, the band came close to breaking up at this point and Waters has said the album could just as easily have been called 'Wish *We* Were Here'. Nevertheless, Wright and Gilmour both now cite it as their favourite Floyd album.

The sleeve design, another triumph for Hipgnosis, has never been adequately transferred to CD. Initially, the album came in a black polythene wrapper with a sticker of George Hardie's shaking robot-hands over a background divided into four segments, depicting the four elements, Earth, Air, Fire and Water (this was the basis of the cover of the first UK CD). Inside the bag was a regular album sleeve with an inner bag. Each of the four faces depicted one of the elements, combined with someone who was "not there".

The burning man (fire) is obviously absent, as he does not feel the heat. The character in the desert (earth) has no face and no arms inside his sleeves. The scarf billowing in the wind (air) concealed a barely visible naked female figure (a different version is used in the reissued CD's booklet), and the diver (water, again different on the new CD) makes no splash. The burning man was used on the front of CDs outside the UK, and the second UK CD release. Also missing from the CDs are the "frame breaks" – each of the four pictures originally spilled onto the surrounding area. Vinyl copies included a free postcard, depicting the splash-less diver. To complicate matters, even vinyl copies differ, with some territories using alternative photos of the burning man.

A quadrophonic version of the album (Harvest Q4SHVL 814) was released, although there are fewer differences between it and the stereo release than is the case with the ATOM HEART MOTHER or DARK SIDE quad remixes. The album has also been available as two different picture discs and on a variety of coloured vinyls.

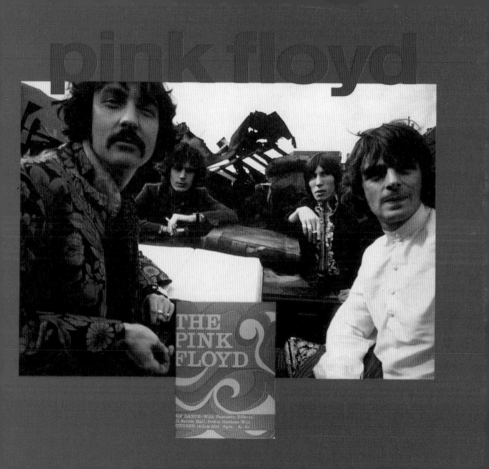

SHINE ON YOU CRAZY DIAMOND (PART 1)
(WATERS/WRIGHT/GILMOUR)

Premièred in France in June 1974, as one long piece, 'Shine On...' was one of three new tracks. The others, 'Raving And Drooling' and Gotta Be Crazy' were held over for 'Animals', where they would resurface with new titles. 'Shine On...', meanwhile, became the centre-piece of the album, divided into two suites to bookend the three conventional songs.

Initially inspired by Gilmour's melancholy guitar theme, the piece is also full of Wright's best ever keyboard work. Another of the track's high points is again Dick Parry's elo-quent saxophone. The lyrics match the poignant sadness of the music and are unmis-takably about Syd Barrett – the only lyric in his *oeuvre* which Waters will admit refers directly to his former band-mate. During final mixing of the track, a balding, portly figure visited the band in the studio. No-one recognised him for some time, thinking he was an EMI engineer, until eventually the penny dropped – it was Syd. As the band repeatedly played back the tape, trying to establish the best mix, he asked

innocently "Why bother? You've heard it once already."

The recording of the track was fraught with more down-to-earth problems as well. The band decided that the first version was not good enough, so after several days wasted work, began recording a second. When this was half done, they were dismayed to find that someone had inadvertently switched echo onto two of the tracks, rendering them use-less, and work had to begin once again.

Confusingly, vinyl copies of the album sub-divided this track into Parts 1-5, with writing credits and start times as follows: Part 1 (Wright/ Waters/ Gilmour); Part 2 (Gilmour/ Waters/ Wright; 2'09"); Part 3 (Waters/ Gilmour/ Wright; 3'54"); Part 4 (Gilmour/ Wright/ Waters; 6'27") Part 5 (Waters; 8'42"). The vocals are, therefore, all in Part 5.

Buried somewhere within 'Shine On...' is part of the abortive 'Household Objects' album with which the band had originally intended to follow 'Dark Side'. This was recorded without the use of any musical instruments, and the band spent hours of stu-dio time tuning strips of sticky tape and wine-glasses full of water – none of which would have been necessary had the Fairlight Synthesiser existed in 1975.

Both parts of 'Shine On...' remained in the set list until the end of the 1977 tour. Parts 1-5 were performed throughout the 1987/9 tour, and included on the 'Delicate Sound Of Thunder' album. They were also played at Knebworth in 1990 and again on the 1994 tour.

WELCOME TO THE MACHINE
(WATERS)

Waters brought these verses to the studio, where writing was completed, making much use of his beloved VCS3 synthesiser. The track was then performed on the 1977 'Animals' tour, during Waters' solo shows and at most of Pink Floyd's post-Waters gigs.

The band usually refer to this as 'The Machine Song', suggesting that this may have been its working title.

HAVE A CIGAR
(WATERS)

Since this was first performed live in April 1975, sung by Waters, it is not unreasonable to suppose it was written during one of the early studio sessions for the album. When

Waters had trouble singing the tune, and Gilmour declined the chore in view of the "complaining" lyric (if only he'd known what was to come!), Waters suggested bringing in Roy Harper, a fellow Harvest artist and friend, for whose 'HQ' album Gilmour had already provided guitar services. Waters later regretted the decision "not because he did it badly... it just isn't us any more". Even so, the song was deemed worthy of release as a single in mainland Europe, Japan and the US. Harper sang it but once again, joining Pink Floyd onstage at the 1975 Knebworth Festival.

In 1987 Waters again deferred vocal duties, this time to "Ace Mechanic" Paul Carrack, who guested throughout the 'Radio KAOS' tour.

The line "Which one's Pink?" really was uttered by an ignorant US record company executive and became a weapon post-split, when Waters used it on one of his tour T-shirts.

WISH YOU WERE HERE
(WATERS/GILMOUR)

Unusually for the Floyd, the lyrics to this melancholy song, sung by Gilmour, were written before the music, although the piece was not heard by a concert audience for sixteen months after the album's release.

The segue from the preceding track, made to sound like a cheap transistor radio, is responsible for apoplexy in more than one unsuspecting hi-fi buff. It was recreated live by the not inconsiderable feat of moving dozens of mixing desk sliders simultaneously.

Classical and jazz violinist Stephane Grapelli made an uncredited contribution, being paid £300 for playing just a few bars, which are barely audible during the closing wind noises. He was used for the simple expedient that he was handy, being in the process of recording in an adjacent studio at Abbey Road. The orchestral snippet was lifted from a recording of Tchaikovsky's Fourth Symphony.

Despite its belated début, the song soon became a live regular, performed after the split by both Waters and Pink Floyd.

SHINE ON YOU CRAZY DIAMOND (PART 2).
(WATERS/WRIGHT/GILMOUR)

A continuation of Part 1, which opened the album. The piece was initially performed whole, but was split in 1975, when 'Have A Cigar' made its début. On vinyl copies, this was subdivided into: Part 6 (Wright/Waters/Gilmour); Part 7 (Waters/Gilmour/Wright; 4'55"); Part 8 (Gilmour/Waters/Wright; 6'24"); Part 9 (Wright – his last ever solo composition for the band, and his last of any kind until 1992; 9'03"). The lyrics from Part 7 were added to performances on the later dates of the 1994 tour.

animals

**EMI 8 29748 2; originally Harvest SHVL 815;
first issued on CD as Harvest CDP 7 46128 2,
released: January 23 1977**

UK Chart: No. 2; US Chart: No. 2

This album, which would turn London's Battersea Power Station into an unlikely tourist attraction, came about when Pink Floyd returned to the two songs discarded during the 'Wish You Were Here' sessions. Assembling at their new North London Studio, Britannia Row, they reworked the songs, plus another Waters had written, about pigs. This gave him the idea for another grand concept, the album's Orwellian, anthropomorphic theme, likening human beings to species of animals. All that was then required was to re-title the songs, revise the lyrics to fit and add a short prelude and finale to bookend the album, not forgetting a few farmyard sounds to give atmosphere. Because of the success of the 'British Winter Tour '74' bootleg, this would be the last time that Pink Floyd would record material that had already been tested on the road.

To many people, the most famous thing about the album is its sleeve, for which Waters had the idea of photographing a flying pig (at least, an inflatable one) over the aforesaid power station. Waters has, inexplicably, described the flying pig as a "symbol of hope". The sleeve required two days to photograph, on the second of which, the pig broke free from its moorings and floated off into the distance, generating many column inches of useful publicity. Of course, there is no reason to suggest that this was anything but an "accident".

Ironically, the resulting photo was not deemed suitable for the sleeve (although several shots are used in the reissue's booklet), so Hipgnosis reverted to their original idea of pasting a shot of the pig onto another of the power station. Waters gave himself credit for the sleeve design, much to the chagrin of Thorgerson, resulting in a rift that kept Hipgnosis from designing sleeves for 'The Wall' and 'The Final Cut'. The dust jacket and CD booklet feature lyrics written out in Nick Mason's own fair hand.

The length of the three main tracks has prevented them from featuring in post-Waters Floyd concerts, although the tour that supported the album, dubbed "Pink Floyd – In The Flesh", where the album was performed in its entirety, was the biggest Pink Floyd ever performed with Waters in the band. They were augmented by a flying inflatable pig and rhythm guitarist Snowy White, who was also allowed to take the occasional solo. On the final date of the tour, Gilmour was so dissatisfied with the band's performance that he watched the encore, a one-off, twelve-minute blues led by White, from the mixing desk. Waters also hated the concert, but it did give him an idea, as we shall see...

PIGS ON THE WING 1
(WATERS)

One of the most personal things ever recorded by Pink Floyd or its solo members, this is a simple love song for Waters' (then) wife Carolyne and is therefore sung by Waters. Both it and its counterpart which closes the album sit in stark contrast to the heavyweight material between them. To further confuse matters, the third line was originally part of 'Raving And Drooling'.

The acoustic nature of the song made it unsuitable as a concert opener for the tour, so the album was performed out of sequence. It also featured in Waters' 84/85 tour, when it was accompanied by back-projected film of the pig over Battersea Power Station, but has not been performed since Waters split from Carolyne.

DOGS
(WATERS/GILMOUR)

A revised version of 'Gotta Be Crazy', a track which constantly evolved over the two years during which it was performed, even before being rewritten for this album. Waters' vitriolic

attack on corporate climbers refers again to a metaphorical stone dragging down its victim, and his love of lists surfaces once more in the final verse.

The vocals are by Gilmour on the first four verses and by Waters on the remaining three. Unsurprisingly, given the writing credits, it is this track which is the album's showcase for Gilmour's guitar, which rises admirably to the occasion. Indeed, fans of his playing often cite this as the ultimate Pink Floyd number, although it was not recorded as easily as it could have been. The problems of self-producing the album in a new studio became apparent when an entire guitar part, of which Gilmour was justifiably very proud, was accidentally wiped by Waters and had to be re-done.

PIGS
(THREE DIFFERENT ONES)
(WATERS)

Waters sees pigs as the people who think they know what's best for others, including Mary Whitehouse, the campaigner for TV censorship and religious bigot, referred to in the third verse.

All the vocals on this song are Waters' and all are electronically treated, but none so much as the Vocoder section after the second verse. Undaunted by what happened to his work on 'Dogs', Gilmour provides another climactic solo.

As one of the numbers written especially for the album, this was only ever performed by Pink Floyd on the '77 tour, although Waters included a truncated version in a medley on his 1987 tour.

SHEEP
(WATERS)

In 1974, 'Sheep' was known as 'Raving And Drooling', sometimes introduced with the unwieldy title of 'Raving And Drooling I Fell On His Neck With A Scream', which was, in fact, its opening line, a lyric whose last vestiges are now found in the penultimate verse. If we're led by dogs and pigs, Waters suggests, then most of us are sheep, blindly working our way towards an early grave, without questioning the systems which govern our existence. Such neo-Marxism is no doubt rooted in his socialist upbringing.

If 'Dogs' was Gilmour's guitar masterpiece,

then 'Sheep' is held together by the bass part, although Gilmour claims to have performed this too. The cleverly rewritten 23rd Psalm was originally performed by Nick Mason, although the version used on the album was recited by an uncredited member of the Floyd's support crew.

'Sheep' came close to being included in Pink Floyd's 1987 comeback tour, but Gilmour felt he couldn't sing Waters' vocal part with sufficient venom. It was, though, included on the 'Great Dance Songs' compilation.

PIGS ON THE WING 2
(WATERS)

Effectively the second verse of the album's opener, Waters used this short song to ensure that the otherwise doom-laden album ended on a positive note.

When the album was issued in the USA as an 8-track cartridge, utilising a continuous tape loop, a bridge was needed so that Part 2 could be segued straight after Part 1. David Gilmour declined the job, offering it instead to Snowy White.

the wall

**EMI/ Harvest 8 31243 2; originally Harvest SHDW 411;
first issued on CD as Harvest CDS 7 46036 8,
released: November 30 1979**

UK Chart: No. 3; US Chart: No. 1
Movie Version: Channel 5 Video CFV 08762

On the final date of the tour which promoted 'Animals', Roger Waters was so enraged by the rowdy behaviour of a front-row fan that he beckoned him forward and spat in the unsuspecting fellow's face. Horrified by his own aggression, Waters began to put together a concept album about his feelings of isolation from his audience and the barriers which potentially exist between all of us. 'The Wall' is the result. Waters started work on the project in September 1977, just two months after the tour had ended. From the beginning, he planned it not merely as an album, but a theatrical concert and movie. The following July, he offered his band mates a choice of two very crude demo recordings – one was 'The Wall', the other, which the rest of the band felt was too personal, eventually became Waters' first genuinely solo album, 'The Pros And Cons Of Hitch Hiking'.

Recording began in April 1979, mostly taking place at Superbear Studios in France (used by Gilmour and Wright for their solo albums the previous year), CBS in New York and The Producers Workshop in LA. Some work was also done at Pink Floyd's (later Nick Mason's) studio at Britannia Row, London, but this was not declared, for company tax reasons, as the band were in dire straits financially, following the collapse of accountants Norton-Warburg, with whom they had invested vast sums of money.

Production credits were shared by Bob Ezrin, David Gilmour and Roger Waters, with

James Guthrie listed as co-producer. Neither the sleeve nor labels of initial copies carried any mention of Wright or Mason, an oversight which was speedily corrected for subsequent pressings. The album featured many uncredited session players with Ezrin and Gilmour covering for Rick Wright, whose input was minimal to begin with and lessened as time progressed. Near the end of recording, Waters gave the others an ultimatum: either Wright quit the band, or he would scrap the project, meaning none of them would recoup their Norton-Warburg losses. Wright reluctantly agreed, was only allowed to perform the live shows on a wage and was the only member of the band not present at the film's World Premier on July 14, 1982.

Breaking with tradition, Hipgnosis were passed over in favour of political cartoonist Gerald Scarfe, designer of the animated back-projections for the 'Wish You Were Here' tour. He was commissioned not only to design the album sleeve, but also puppets for the stage show and animated films for promo video, concert and movie. Although the sleeve was devoid of lettering of any sort, a transparent, removable plastic label indicated the record's identity. Contrary to the claim of the generic sticker affixed to the 1994 reissue, its booklet does not include photographs, let alone "additional" ones, although the lyrics are printed in a larger, more readable size. A more notable quirk of the re-issue is that the tracks are indexed to begin and end in different places to the first CD. This is because rather than clean breaks between songs, there are frequently segues comprising pieces of *musique concrète* which could belong to either track.

The concerts remain the most spectacular ever staged by a rock band. As they played, a wall of cardboard bricks was built across the stage in front of them, meaning that they performed half of the show hidden from view. The wall doubled as a screen, onto which were projected images, including Scarfe's animations. The trademark aeroplane, which crashed into the stage in a ball of flame, reappeared, as did the flying pig. The stage was also shared with forty-foot high puppets.

Owing to the complexity and cost of the stage show, 'The Wall' was performed in only four cities: New York and Los Angeles in February 1980, London in August 1980, and

Dortmund in February 1981. Further London concerts followed in June 1981, to allow for filming. Although the resulting films have never been seen publicly (at least, not legally) the intention was to include scenes in the movie version, which was directed by Alan Parker to Roger Waters' screenplay. Production of the film was to become a headache as Waters, Scarfe and Parker clashed over their interpretation of the screenplay. Parker, as director, had the final say, although all three regard the film as something of a compromise.

In 1990, Waters performed 'The Wall' once more, in Berlin, with an all-star cast, to raise funds for the Memorial Fund for Disaster Relief.

In the summer of 1994, he announced that he was rewriting 'The Wall' as a stage musical.

'The Wall' examines the barriers that we all – and specifically the tale's hero, a rock star referred to as both "Pink" and "Mr. Floyd" – build around ourselves to deflect criticism and to avoid facing up to our own failures. It describes Pink's breakdown as he sits in a hotel room during an American tour, and the concert he performs that night. It is partly autobiographical, partly about Barrett's decline and partly fiction, with a few incidents no doubt drawn from rock'n'roll folklore. The traditional disclaimer, seen at the end of the film, that "Any similarity to actual persons...

is coincidental" can therefore be taken with a pinch of salt.

Perhaps understandably, the story has been described as over-convoluted and disjointed. Right up until the last minute, tracks were being both rearranged, to keep the story coherent, and cut, to keep the threatened triple album down to a cost-effective double. It is certainly easier to follow the film if you are already familiar with the album, although, conversely, some aspects of the story are clearer on screen. It helps to realise that most of the story is told or seen in flash-back, except for the scenes in Pink's hotel room and the subsequent concert, which Pink thinks is a Fascist rally.

Since Waters originally conceived the stage show and film at the same time as the record, it would not be right to consider any one of them in isolation.

WHEN THE TIGERS BROKE FREE
(WATERS)

Although written for the album, describing the death of Waters' father at the Anzio Beachhead, one of the killing grounds of the Allied campaign in Italy in January 1944, this

first reached its public when the first verse was used as the opening number of the film. The second and third verses were used after 'Another Brick In The Wall, Part 1'.

It was also released (as Harvest HAR 5222, in a superb fold-out sleeve with film stills) as a teaser single for 'The Final Cut' when that album was still intended to be a collection of 'Wall' out-takes and soundtrack material.

IN THE FLESH?
(WATERS)

The record opens with the barely audible words "we came in", which hardly make sense until, during the dying moments some eighty minutes later, one hears "Isn't this where". The opening bars of music also mirror the final track, while the last sounds heard are a simulation of the Stuka dive-bomber which kills Pink's father – and which killed Waters' father.

This overture takes its name from 1977's "Pink Floyd – In The Flesh" tour. Technically, the band have never performed the track live, as each concert opened with the four-man "surrogate band" playing, while the real Pink Floyd waited, the audience none-the-wiser, in the wings. In 1980, this band, who also padded out the Floyd sound for the rest of the concert, comprised: guitarist Snowy White, Willie Wilson (drummer in the band with which Gilmour toured France and Spain in the '60s, and on Gilmour's first solo album), Andy Bown (bass) and Peter Woods (keyboards). In 1981, Andy Roberts replaced Snowy White.

Bob Geldof sang the version that was recorded for the film.

THE THIN ICE
(WATERS)

The first flashback is to Pink's birth and childhood. The idea of "the thin ice of modern life" may, perhaps, have been subconsciously influenced by Jethro Tull's 'Skating Away On The Thin Ice Of A New Day' of 1974.

ANOTHER BRICK IN THE WALL, PART 1
(WATERS)

The first "brick" in Pink's wall is the loss of his father, an incident drawn from Waters' own childhood. His pained lyrics are delivered over a bubbling bass riff, with just a few staccato guitar stabs from Gilmour. For his 1987 con-

certs, Waters performed this and the following two songs as one piece. A brief snippet of the number was prefixed to Pink Floyd's 1994 performances of 'Part 2'.

THE HAPPIEST DAYS OF OUR LIVES
(WATERS)

Does anybody believe the hoary old myth that school days are the happiest of our lives? Waters obviously didn't, although he did revive the track for his 1985 and '87 tours.

In the film, Pink is caught red-handed writing poems in class. The teacher recites one, humiliating Pink in the process. It just happens to be the opening verse of 'Money'.

ANOTHER BRICK IN THE WALL, PART 2
(WATERS)

Otherwise articulate critics have used their – mistaken – interpretation of these lyrics as a stick with which to beat Pink Floyd on many occasions. They see a rich, well educated Waters saying that there is no point in educating the masses. In reality, of course, Waters is warning that cruel and vindictive teachers are liable to turn children away from the liberating education that is their birthright.

An obvious choice for a single, 'Another Brick...' was released (as Harvest HAR 5194) in time for Christmas, with a new, eight-second instrumental intro and truncated guitar solo, fading just before the "how can you have any pudding" dialogue. It had the distinction of being the last UK Number One of the Seventies, and the first of the Eighties. It also managed to get itself banned in South Africa, after being adopted as a protest song by schoolchildren in the townships. It made the charts again a year later, as part of a light-hearted Christmas medley of reworded cover versions by the Barron Knights. Waters later collected a British Academy Award (BAFTA) for 'Another Brick...', as "best song from a film". As a result of the single and album's success, Pink Floyd were later inducted into America's National Association of Brick Distributors' Hall Of Fame.

The tabloid press made much from their discovery that the schoolchildren who sang on the chorus had not been paid for their contribution - the deal being that their school would be given free time in Britannia Row for music lessons.

MOTHER
(WATERS)

Waters, who performed the song on his 'Radio Kaos' tour in 1987, has pointed out that it is not an attack on his own mother (a teacher and communist member of CND), but overbearing mothers, and the potential of all mothers to hold back their offspring, in general.

The track used several uncredited session musicians, including an unknown keyboard player, Jeff Porcaro on drums and Lee Ritenour on guitar. A much sparser version was recorded for the film, with some very minor changes to the lyrics.

GOODBYE BLUE SKY
(WATERS)

Initially opening the second side of vinyl, 'Goodbye Blue Sky' mixes acoustic guitar with menacing keyboards and a fine example of Gilmour's pastoral singing, to provide a tranquil interlude after the opening bombast, and an opportunity to reflect on the mental scars carried by Pink at the end of the war. In the film, the track came after the second part of 'When The Tigers Broke Free', to accompany a superb animated sequence.

EMPTY SPACES
(WATERS)

This instrumental was replaced in live performances, and for the film, by 'What Shall We Do Now', which is basically the same tune. The album's notorious backward message occurs here. For the benefit of readers whose CD players only spin anti-clockwise, it says "Congratulations, you have just discovered the secret message. Send your answer to Old Pink, care of The Funny Farm, Chalfont". The first CD issue mistakenly indexed this track and 'Young Lust' as one item.

WHAT SHALL WE DO NOW
(WATERS)

Observant readers will notice that his song – another of Waters' list-like lyrics – is not heard on the album. It was dropped at the last minute, as material was re-sequenced and cut to prevent the double album from becoming a triple, but too late to have the lyrics removed from the sleeve, which was already at the printers (they have been incised from all CD versions). It was, though, used at this point at the concerts and in the film, where it accompanied more of Scarfe's animation. Originally, it came later in the story.

YOUNG LUST
(WATERS/GILMOUR)

Waters asked Gilmour to repeat his vocal performance from 'The Nile Song' for this "pastiche of just any rock'n'roll band out on the road", a situation in which Pink discovers groupies. Cinematographic train-spotters should note an early appearance by Joanne Whalley, as the only one of the groupies to keep her vest on.

The 'phone call where Pink's wife's lover answers the 'phone and then hangs up was staged, but the telephone operator is real and was unaware of the situation - all her comments were made under the impression that the call was genuine.

ONE OF MY TURNS
(WATERS)

Disgusted with his treatment of a groupie, and at the same time saddened by his wife's infidelity and the disintegration of their marriage, Pink throws a wobbly, trashing his hotel room. During the film, "The Dambusters" plays on

THE WALL : PINK FLOYD

Pink's T.V. at this point. One of the original Dambusters' pilots was Leonard Cheshire, founder of the charity for which Waters performed 'The Wall' in Berlin in 1990.

The uncredited rhythm guitar was by Lee Ritenour, because, as Gilmour put it, he "couldn't think of a good part to play". The groupie's voice was originally to be provided by Roger. Thankfully, Bob Ezrin found a woman willing to re-do the part. The song was a surprising choice for the B-side of the 'Another Brick...' single.

The original CD indexed this as two tracks, breaking as the mood suddenly changes midway through, while a typographical error on the label of some copies names the track 'One Of My Tunes'!

DON'T LEAVE ME NOW
(WATERS)

Like many needy and selfish men, Pink is unable to understand why his wife leaves him, even though he catalogues the many abysmal ways he has treated her.

The film mixes action footage with the sort of animation that would have given Freud a field day.

ANOTHER BRICK IN THE WALL, PART 3
(WATERS)

Rejected, Pink declares that he doesn't need anything people have to offer him.

Live performances, particularly during the second round of 'Wall' concerts, included an extended instrumental ending. A more up-tempo rendition is heard in the film.

GOODBYE CRUEL WORLD
(WATERS)

The wall around Pink is complete: he has isolated himself, totally, from his friends and loved ones. This ends the first half of the record and concert, and marked the insertion of the last brick in the physical wall which separated the band from audience.

The octave performed on the bass is a Waters favourite, harking back to 'Careful With That Axe, Eugene'.

HEY YOU
(WATERS)

The fact that these lyrics appeared in the wrong place on the original album sleeve was another indication of the last minute re-sequencing which took place as Bob Ezrin strove to keep the album within four sides of vinyl, and make sense of the story. The song, which had fretless bass played by David Gilmour, was cut completely from the film version, even though it had accompanied scenes of rioting and looting in the early rushes. Stills from these scenes can be seen in the long-deleted photo-book which accompanied the film, *Pink Floyd – The Wall* (Avon, 1982).

When 'The Wall' was performed live, 'Hey You' was played at the end of the interval, with no warning - the house lights were still up and the band were hidden behind the wall.

Waters performed 'Hey You' during his 1984/5 concerts and it was used as an encore during the 1994 Pink Floyd Tour.

IS THERE ANYBODY OUT THERE?
(WATERS)

Too late, Pink realises his predicament.

David Gilmour admitted defeat and brought in a session musician to play the Spanish guitar, which he said he could play with a leather pick, but not with his fingers, as it should be done. He also says that Ezrin should have received a co-composition credit for his contribution. The "seagull" noises could have come straight from the middle of 'Echoes', while the dialogue was lifted from an episode of the US Western serial *Gunsmoke*, called *Fandango*. The subtle use of a string section is also noteworthy, as it portends things to come.

Roger Waters later reworked the track (adding even more bone-chilling screams) for use in a cinema commercial for The Samaritans, which ended with the comforting caption "Yes".

NOBODY HOME
(WATERS)

Still in his hotel room, Pink reflects on his situation. The line about "elastic bands keeping my shoes on" is a direct reference to Syd Barrett's behaviour during his final weeks with Pink Floyd. Similarly, the "grand piano to prop up my mortal remains" was said to be a dig at Rick Wright.

Performing the song live (which he also did on his 'Pros & Cons' and 'KAOS' tours), Roger Waters appeared in a gap in the wall, in a "hotel room" with a table, chair, standard lamp and television. He would switch channels on the latter, which could clearly be heard over the P.A.

VERA
(WATERS)

Flashing back to the end of the war, Pink feels betrayed by his father's failure to return, even though "forces' sweetheart" Vera Lynn had promised "We'll meet again, some sunny day". Lynn's 'The Little Boy That Santa Claus Forgot' is heard at the beginning of the film.

BRING THE BOYS BACK HOME
(WATERS)

Joe Porcaro (father of Jeff) plays snare.

A version of this, completely re-recorded for the film with the addition of the Pontarddulais Male Voice Choir, was used as the B-side of 'When The Tigers Broke Free'.

COMFORTABLY NUMB
(WATERS/GILMOUR)

Pink's manager (a brilliant cameo in the film from Bob Hoskins, who speaks volumes with his two words of dialogue) arrives to escort

Pink to the concert, but of course Pink is in no state to attend. Concerned only for the financial situation, the manager fetches a doctor who injects Pink with something to "keep him going". This relates to a real incident when Waters was persuaded to play a gig, despite suffering the effects of being prescribed strong drugs for what turned out to be hepatitis.

Waters' words were put to a tune which David Gilmour had written at the end of sessions for his eponymous 1978 solo album. Gilmour aired a short section of his original demo on Nicky Horne's radio show in July 1992. The released version is an amalgam of the two takes the band recorded: a tight version favoured by Gilmour and the looser cut preferred by Waters and Ezrin.

A vehicle for Gilmour's most blistering guitar solo, 'Come On Big Bum' (as he refers to it privately) has since become a live favourite, being performed during his 1984 solo shows (one of only three Pink Floyd songs he used) with Mick Ralphs handling Waters' lines, and, on one notable occasion, Mason guesting on drums. Ralphs also joined Gilmour on a version performed to raise funds for disaster relief, available on the *Columbian Volcano*

Concert video (Hendring HEN 2 086), with, among others, Sam Brown on backing vocals and Michael Kamen on keyboards. Pink Floyd performed the number on their 1987-9 and 1994 tours and in 1987 Roger Waters received so many requests for it from fans that he promised to include it the next time he went on the road. He kept his word by performing the track at the Guitar Legends festival in Seville in September 1991.

THE SHOW MUST GO ON
(WATERS)

Waters had wanted this to sound "like" The Beach Boys and, in typical Pink Floyd fashion, (i.e. nothing but the best) booked The Beach Boys themselves to record the vocals. This plan backfired when they decided the themes of the album didn't fit their carefully nurtured (but completely false) wholesome image, and went off to do their own tour instead. The desired effect was achieved by recruiting Bruce Johnston (who replaced Brian Wilson in The Beach Boys in 1965), Joe Chemay (who has worked as a session singer with The Beach Boys), Stan Farber, Jim Haas and John Joyce. Other than Johnston, they all appeared

at 'The Wall' concerts, including Waters' Berlin bash. Chemay, Haas and Joyce also made a guest appearance at one of Waters' 1987 concerts.

Originally indexed to run for thirty-five seconds, the 1994 CD gives this track just thirty (thirty-one on the version in the 'Shine On' box set), making it the shortest piece recorded by the band.

Live versions included the extra lyrics which, although on the original sleeve, had been cut from the album in yet another attempt to reduce the running time. However, the number was omitted from the film.

IN THE FLESH
(WATERS)

Pink arrives at the concert, but thinks he is a Fascist leader, addressing a rally. This is the same point in the narrative as where the album opened, and the song reprises the album's opening number (note the disappearing question mark). Hammond Organ was provided by Freddie Mandell, while Bob Geldof again sang for the film.

Although clearly a work of fiction, the lyrics in this and the following two songs have often been appropriated by those sad individuals who would adopt such policies in real life, to the point where racist graffiti in Liverpool in 1987 was accompanied by the crossed-hammers logo used in the film. Even many of the (real) skinhead extras involved in the film did not accept that Geldof was acting.

Nevertheless, Roger Waters performed the track with great relish during his solo tours.

RUN LIKE HELL
(WATERS/GILMOUR)

On first hearing, the sparse bass and guitar intro and the fixed disco-ish, military-style 2/4 rhythm of this song make it seem over simple, but the pace is ideally suited to the menacing lyrics, as Waters was surely aware.

At the original Wall concerts, where it provided a musical backdrop for the reappearance of the flying pig, Waters took great delight in introducing this as 'Run Like Fuck', dedicating it to "all the paranoids in the audience".

This is a particular favourite of David Gilmour, who again wrote the music while working on his solo album in 1978. He performed it on his '84 solo tour and it is also on the *Columbia Volcano Concert* video. Pink

Floyd performed it on their 1987-9 tour and at Knebworth '90, using a recording from Atlanta, November '87 as the B-side of 'On The Turning Away'. Roger Waters responded by releasing a 'Potsdamer' mix of the track on the B-side of his live 'Another Brick In The Wall' single from Berlin. This was a truly awful dance version with tacked-on live applause.

Instrumental extracts were used in the *La Carrera Panamericana* soundtrack and the song was played again on Pink Floyd's 1994 tour, with Guy Pratt handling Waters' vocal parts. He would replace the "...send you back to mother in a cardboard box" lyric with "...send you back to New York...", or wherever the band happened to be playing.

WAITING FOR THE WORMS
(WATERS)

As the Fascists go onto the streets, Pink (Waters, in the studio) uses a megaphone to describe the route of a right-wing march through racially-mixed areas of London, into Hyde Park. Note the strange laughter on the right-hand channel at about 2'24".

In Waters' demo version of the album, "The

Worms" - a symbol of moral and mental decay - played a much greater part in the story.

STOP
(WATERS)

Pink finally starts to question what he has become.

In the film, the solitary verse is read by Pink, from a book of his poetry. He recites other "poems", some of which would resurface in 'Your Possible Pasts' on 'The Final Cut', and '5.11 AM (The Moment Of Clarity)' on Waters' 'The Pros And Cons Of Hitch Hiking'.

THE TRIAL
(WATERS/EZRIN)

In order to save himself, Pink puts himself on trial. He is his own prosecutor, judge and jury. The only possible punishment, and his salvation, is to tear down the wall, face up to his position and resume his interaction with society. The scream which accompanies the disintegration of the wall in the film makes obvious the fact that this is not an easy thing for Pink to do.

The song, co-written with Ezrin, is hammed up by Waters in the style of a Gilbert and Sullivan operetta. After the judge's comment that he is filled "with the urge to defecate", a voice shouts "go on judge, sit on it!".

OUTSIDE THE WALL
(WATERS)

The album's coda is best explained in Roger Waters' own words: "That final song is saying 'Right, well, that was it, you've seen it now. That's the best we can do, really. And that wasn't actually us. This is us. That was us performing a piece of theatre about the things that it was about and we do like you really'."

This was re-recorded for the film, again with the Pontarddulais Male Voice Choir. Live performances included a variety of musical treats, differing from night to night, including Nick Mason on acoustic guitar and David Gilmour on mandolin.

a collection of great dance songs

EMI CDP 7 90732 2; originally Harvest SHVL 822, released: November 23 1981

UK Chart: No. 37; US Chart: No. 31

Hastily compiled by David Gilmour as a contractual gap-filler and released with the Christmas market in mind, this greatest hits collection still interests fans by virtue of the inclusion of several alternative versions of the well known songs it contains.

The cover was again provided by Thorgerson and, like the title, is a play on Nick Mason's joke that their US record company probably thought of Pink Floyd as a dance band. In a similarly jocular vein, Gilmour has said of the artwork "it was so awful, I thought I'd get it cheap".

ONE OF THESE DAYS
(GILMOUR/MASON/WRIGHT/WATERS)
The standard album version.

MONEY
(WATERS)
The unavailability of the original version, due to a change in US record company after 'Dark Side...', meant that David Gilmour had to re-record the track. He acted as producer and played everything, other than saxophone, which was again provided by Dick Parry. James Guthrie co-produced and mixed. Even the original till ringing and rattling coin effects were

used. An edited cut of the new version was scheduled for release as a single, to coincide with the album, to the point where a catalogue number (Harvest HAR 5217) was allocated and its B-side, 'Let There Be More Light', announced. The idea was abandoned at the last minute, but not before some pink vinyl promo copies had escaped into the collectors' market.

SHEEP
(WATERS)

The 'Animals' version, probably selected as it is the shortest of the three key songs on that album, although Gilmour has said he had "quite a lot" to do with how it had evolved and was "quite proud" of it.

SHINE ON YOU CRAZY DIAMOND
(GILMOUR/WATERS/WRIGHT)

This is a composite version, segueing Parts 1, 2, 3, 5, and 7 of the original, but with the last two minutes, the sax break, cut from Part 5. By editing together the two pieces from 'Wish You Were Here' in this way, the piece was restored to something resembling the original version as first performed in 1974.

WISH YOU WERE HERE
(GILMOUR/WATERS)

The original album version, but with a slightly trimmed intro and outro.

ANOTHER BRICK IN THE WALL PART 2
(WATERS)

Uses the intro from the single version, but the album cut's ending.

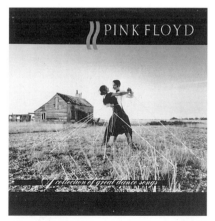

the final cut

**EMI/ Harvest 8 31242 2; originally Harvest SHPF 1983;
first issued on CD as Harvest CDP 7 446129 2,
released: March 21 1983**

UK Chart: No. 1; US Chart: No. 6

The band's (or at least, Roger Waters') original intention had been that 'The Final Cut' would be a soundtrack album to The Wall movie (one unimaginative working title was 'Spare Bricks'), with the non-album and re-recorded tracks from the film plus some new material. Indeed, this was how it was first announced to the press. The film's credits also claim that a soundtrack album is available, while the label of 'When The Tigers Broke Free' states that it is "from 'The Final Cut'."

By the time it was released, though, it had developed into a full blown concept album, fuelled by Waters' rows with film director Alan Parker, the Falklands conflict and its composer's despair at the state of Thatcherite Britain. For this was, in all but name, a Roger Waters solo album. David Gilmour has openly admitted so, relinquishing his right to a producer's credit (but not the accompanying royalty share!), and has gone so far as to say that there are only three good tracks on it. He was particularly unhappy at the inclusion of tracks which were rejected, allegedly on quality grounds, from 'The Wall'.

Andy Bown, who had contributed to 'The Wall' concerts, replaced Rick Wright on keyboards. Piano and harmonium were added by Michael Kamen, who earned a production credit for his work arranging the National Philharmonic Orchestra, the other producers being Waters and James Guthrie. Ubiquitous percussionist Ray Cooper also contributed. Among the eight studios used, all in England, were Hook End, then

Gilmour's home, and The Billiard Room, at Waters' London residence.

The recording sessions became more and more fraught as time went on, Waters being determined not to compromise, as he no doubt felt he had during filming of 'The Wall', while Gilmour and Mason seemed to become, to him, mere session musicians.

Despite reaching the top of the UK charts (something neither 'Dark Side...' nor 'The Wall' achieved) the album failed to sell on the scale

of its predecessors, perhaps because the proposed live shows to support it never emerged. Although Waters has performed parts, the recent incarnation of Pink Floyd appear to have completely disowned it. It comes as no surprise that they have never performed any of it in concert, but the decision, against Waters' strong protests, to exclude it from the 'Shine On' box set is less understandable. The 1994 re-issue suffers the same adjustments to track-lengths as 'The Wall', but the only extra photograph is the one on the CD label.

The album's special effects utilised Holophonic sound, a recording technique which accurately captures three-dimensional movement. For best results, listeners should wear headphones, and close their eyes. It really does work, honest.

The album sleeve, depicting a war veteran's jacket in close up, with medal ribbons and part of a poppy, was designed by Waters and photographed by his wife Carolyne's brother, Willie Christie. The album's subtitle, "A Requiem For The Post War Dream By Roger Waters, Performed By Pink Floyd", underlined his almost total control over the project. Even so, the irony of such a strongly anti-war album being put out by a label belonging to Thorn EMI, one of the world's largest arms manufacturers, seems to have been lost on him.

The 'solo' nature of the work was emphasised by the subsequent "Video E.P.", in which Waters is the only member of the band seen – albeit hidden by shadow. The four track EP (Video Music Collection PM 0010) was directed, to a screenplay by Waters, by Christie. Interestingly, the EP comprised the album's lead single and the three tracks thought by Gilmour to be up to scratch.

THE POST WAR DREAM
(WATERS)

The album opens with its central character ("The Hero") listening to the news on his car radio, including an announcement that the replacement for *The Atlantic Conveyer*, a container ship lost in the Falklands campaign with 24 men, will be built in Japan, not in a British yard as had been hoped. (This scene is used at the start of the Video EP, although the track itself is not.)

Having said that, the first verse is very much in the first person, Waters' again referring to the death of his own father. His unfortunate use of the colloquial name for the

Japanese, 'Nips', and the suggestions that "all their kids [commit] suicide" attracted criticisms of racism.

The references to 'Maggie' are, of course, aimed at Margaret Thatcher, the long running Tory Prime Minister, architect of the Falklands campaign and more often the target of songwriters like Billy Bragg than a millionaire rock star.

Michael Kamen's brass-heavy orchestrations add weight to the track.

YOUR POSSIBLE PASTS
(WATERS)

The clanking of railway wagons, intended to suggest the cattle trucks (also referred to in the lyrics) which took Jews, Gypsies, homosexuals, disabled people and dissidents to German concentration camps before and during the war, are recorded Holophonically.

A heavy Gilmour guitar solo is the only musical colour in Waters' sparse landscape, and although this is a rewrite of one of the songs rejected for 'The Wall', it is a perfect vehicle for the sombre subject. The lyrics printed on the sleeve and CD booklet include a couplet which is not sung.

ONE OF THE FEW
(WATERS)

The character in this short bridge piece, and the next song, is the teacher from 'The Wall' who, we now learn, is a war hero, returned to civilian society. The song's working title was 'Teach'. It is yet another example of Waters' technique of using lists for song lyrics, taking its title from Winston Churchill's famous speech about RAF pilots after the Battle Of Britain: "Never, in the field of human conflict, was so much owed, by so many, to so few".

THE HERO'S RETURN
(WATERS)

The "Hero", we also learn, is tormented by memories of the death of one of his air-crew, the gunner, and is unable to discuss this with his wife.

Despite being another reject from 'The Wall', this was used as the B-side to 'Not Now John', listed as "Parts I&II", the second part being an extra verse, not heard on the album. Sadly, the chance to add the extra material to the re-mastered CD was passed up.

THE GUNNERS DREAM
(WATERS)

The Gunner's – and indeed, the post war – dream was of a world free of fear and tyranny, on a large or small scale, where the elderly can walk the streets in safety, where no-one need fear secret police or terrorists (the latter evidenced by reference to the IRA's bloody 1981 attack on army bandsmen in Hyde Park).The penultimate verse is the voice of "The Hero". A superb sax break by Raf 'Baker Street' Ravenscroft is one of the album's musical highlights, no doubt helping to make this one of the three tracks acceptable to David Gilmour.

The lyric referring to "the corner of some foreign field" is borrowed from a World War I sonnet, "The Soldier", by the poet Rupert Brooke, once a resident of the Grantchester area of Cambridge. The original lines read "If I should die, think only this of me:/That there's some corner of a foreign field/ That is forever England".

Pink Floyd's usual quality control slipped when this track was denied its rightful apostrophe on the album sleeve and labels, an error perpetuated on the CD issue.

The Video E.P. opens with this number, and we see that the hero/ teacher's son was lost in the Falklands. The Hero is played by Alex McAvoy, who played the teacher in *The Wall*, in case anyone has missed the point. Roger Waters' mouth and chin are seen, as is the back of his head, as he talks to a psychiatrist called "A. Parker-Marshall", a name derived from the director of *The Wall* movie, and its producer, Alan Marshall. Waters used the song in his 1984/5 concerts.

PARANOID EYES
(WATERS)

Simply, this is the story of the hero's middle age, hiding from his fears behind alcohol and a "stiff upper lip".

For the first half of the song, the music is almost entirely orchestral.

GET YOUR FILTHY HANDS OFF MY DESERT
(WATERS)

The album's second side opened with the best use of Holophonic recording: a rocket is launched in front of the listener, passes overhead and explodes to the rear.

As if the earlier orchestration wasn't enough, Waters sings the opening verse, describing just a few topical acts of aggression, over a string quartet - a far cry from the psychedelia of 1967!

Waters performed the song on both his 1984/5 and '87 tours.

THE FLETCHER MEMORIAL HOME
(WATERS)

The title is a tilt of the hat to Waters' father, Eric Fletcher Waters, to whom the album was dedicated. Waters proposes assembling a host of world leaders – at best inept and at worst corrupt and bloodthirsty – and applying to them the same "final solution" as used by the Nazis in the holocaust.

Another powerful guitar solo explains why this is one of the few tracks on the album liked by David Gilmour.

Used to close the Video EP, its impact is lessened by the comic Napoleon, with his oversize snail. Thatcher and an Argentinian general are also seen arguing over possession of a croquet ball, with Winston Churchill watching on.

SOUTHAMPTON DOCK
(WATERS)

Southampton was the embarkation point for a large number of the men sent to regain the Falkland Islands after the Argentinian invasion. It is also the place to which not quite so many men returned some time later.

The second verse again refers to Maggie Thatcher, as evidenced by Waters lengthening a line in the second verse to "The slippery reins of state" when he performed the song on his 1987 solo tour. He had also performed it in 1985.

THE FINAL CUT
(WATERS)

In the movie industry, "The Final Cut" is the name given to the last edit of a film before the soundtrack is added. Waters uses the term to allude to both suicide and being stabbed in the back - as depicted by the jacket he wore in one of the small pictures on the album's sleeve. This showed him in military uniform, holding film cans, with a cleaver embedded between his shoulder blades - a comment on his relationship with *Wall* director Alan Parker.

Around this time, he also had a jacket made with a knife in the back, which 'bled' theatrical blood as he squeezed a bulb in the pocket.

The lyrics refer to both 'The Wall' and 'Dark Side...' although the reference to the former is only discernible from the printed lyrics, being drowned out by a shotgun blast on the record. Gilmour again stamps his mark of approval in the form of a mellow guitar solo.

On the Video EP the track backs a montage of old, black and white newsreel footage of women at work and play through the ages.

NOT NOW JOHN
(WATERS)

David Gilmour's only vocal on the album is in the guise of another character, someone who wants to bury his head in the sand and not worry about the state of the world. The female backing vocalists are uncredited. The final verse repeats the same line, in broken Italian, pidgin Spanish, schoolboy French and finally Anglo-Saxon English, mimicking the stereotypical British lager lout on holiday in Europe.

'Not Now John' was the only single to be taken from 'The Final Cut' with the chorus suitably overdubbed "Stuff All That". For this reason, the altered recording is sometimes referred to as the "polite" or "obscured" version.

The promo film for the single was the third track on the Video EP, with "typical" lazy British workmen apparently idling away their time, heedless of the threat of competition from Japan. If Waters intended any other meaning, it was lost on most viewers.

Waters performed the song on his 1987 'Radio KAOS' tour.

TWO SUNS IN THE SUNSET
(WATERS)

As the narrator – be he the hero, or Waters himself – drives off into the sunset, in good old cowboy style, he is dazzled by a second sun in his rear view mirror – a nuclear explosion. The children's voices probably belong to Waters' own son and daughter, Harry and India.

The drums were played by Andy Newmark, Nick Mason having had trouble finding the style Waters wanted. Whether he would have felt more inclined to persevere with the track if the atmosphere in the recording studio had been better is a matter for conjecture. Indeed,

it is probable that the final track on the final album Waters recorded under the Pink Floyd banner features no other member of the band. It ends on a sax solo by Ravenscroft.

Unlike previous Pink Floyd concept albums – and, indeed, Waters' subsequent solo work – it is notable that 'The Final Cut' closes in a very down mood indeed. The irony of the album's closing line, "we were all equal in the end" was not lost on those who followed the band's descent into a pit of writs, bitter press releases and catty remarks.

a momentary lapse of reason

EMI CDP 7 48068 2, released: September 7 1987

UK Chart: No. 3; US Chart: No. 3

In 1986, Roger Waters announced to the world that he had left Pink Floyd, which he described as "a spent force creatively", obviously assuming that the band would cease to exist without him. Pink Floyd's management issued a press release to the contrary, announcing their intention to continue regardless. These were the opening shots in the most acrimonious period in the band's history. While Waters busied himself first with abortive threats to block their plans through litigation, then with his solo career, Gilmour and Mason began work on the new Pink Floyd album.

It would take a book many times larger than this to detail all the arguments and counter arguments, but the gist of Waters' complaints (other than to say the band shouldn't continue without him, period) was that the album was an ersatz Pink Floyd, created by an army of "ghost writers" and session musicians. Although Gilmour denied this at the time, in a later interview he made the astonishing admission: "Nick played a few tom-toms on one track, but for the rest I had to get in other drummers. Rick played some tiny little parts. For a lot of it, I played the keyboards and pretended it was him." Even so, Nick Mason now had the distinction of being the only person to play on every Pink Floyd album.

Wright had rejoined his colleagues halfway through the recording sessions, but after taking legal advice decided not to join the band formally, but to remain on a wage. The credits pointedly listed his name in the smaller type used for the army of session musicians, and he is not pictured alongside Gilmour and Mason in the David Bailey portraits included in the album's artwork.

'Lapse' was co-produced by Bob Ezrin and David Gilmour, causing further irritation to Waters, since Ezrin, it was claimed, failed to honour a commitment to produce Waters' 'Radio KAOS' in order to work on the Floyd project. Recording began on Gilmour's houseboat studio, the *Astoria*, then moved to a series of studios in Los Angeles, in order that the album could be completed by session musicians and the band could escape the constant stream of 'phone calls from lawyers preparing to fight Waters. Britannia Row was also used. Waters was replaced by one of the world's leading bass session players, Tony Levin. Pat Leonard, better known for his work with Madonna, contributed synthesiser and Jim Keltner and Carmine Appice both added drums.

Waters' departure also cleared the way for Storm Thorgerson to return to what many considered his rightful place as the Floyd's sleeve designer. His cover for this album is every bit as imaginative, bold and, indeed, expensive, as befits Pink Floyd. He took over Saunton Sands in North Devon for two days, and arranged liter-

ally hundreds of hospital beds along the beach. Although it might have been easier to cheat and retouch his photographs, the line of beds really does snake along the sea-shore for two miles.

Asked what he thought of the album, Waters succinctly described it as "a pretty fair forgery".

SIGNS OF LIFE
(GILMOUR/EZRIN)

Opening with the sound of a rowing boat, this simple guitar and synthesiser instrumental, built around one of Gilmour's 1978 demos, features Nick Mason's spoken voice and sets the tone for the rest of the album. It also came close to being the album's title track, until it was realised that it might be a gift to sarcastic reviewers. It was also used in the *La Carrera Panamericana* soundtrack.

LEARNING TO FLY
(GILMOUR/MOORE/EZRIN/CARIN)

Based around a keyboard instrumental by Jon Carin, this tells the tale of David Gilmour's flying lessons. Already an accomplished pilot (and owner of an impressive fleet of historic aircraft), Gilmour would often absent himself from recording sessions in order to clock up flying hours and add extra, specialist skills to his licence. He allowed Nick Horne to broadcast ninety seconds of Carin's demo during their July 1992 Radio One interview.

Anthony Moore, latterly of Blackhill-managed band Slapp Happy, wrote the lyrics, assisted by Gilmour. To these were added a recording of Nick Mason running through a pre-takeoff checklist. An edited version of the song became the world's first CD-only single, (EMI CD EM 26), although EMI cheated slightly by making pink and black 7" vinyl copies available "for promotional purposes only". Two different promo films were shot by Storm Thorgerson, one of which was also back-projected when the song was performed live.

THE DOGS OF WAR
(GILMOUR/MOORE)

This title is derived from Antony's speech in Shakespeare's *Julius Caesar*, "Cry 'Havoc!' and let slip the dogs of war", via Frederick Forsyth, who used the term as the title of his novel about mercenaries, who are also the subject of this song. The lyrics, which bear no relation to the similarly titled track on 'Animals', were developed by Anthony Moore from an idea outlined by Gilmour, including the line "we all have a dark side", which Gilmour has conceded is a dig at Roger Waters.

One of the worst aspects of this fairly standard rocker is Scott Page's saxophone, truly a low point in Pink Floyd's history. Even so, it became a live regular, a version of which, recorded in Atlanta in November 1987, was used to back some formats of the 'One Slip' single. A promo film for the track was shot at the same concert .

ONE SLIP
(GILMOUR/MANZANERA)

On this occasion, Gilmour's lyrics were put to music by his friend since his early days in Pink Floyd, former Roxy Music guitarist Phil Manzanera. One of the lyrics became the album's title, although this was very much a last-minute decision. Coincidentally (or perhaps not), Manzanera and Pink Floyd are both managed by Steve O'Rourke's company EMKA Productions.

Another *La Carrera Panamericana* tune, 'One Slip' was the third and final single from the album (EMI EM 52) and was to see action on the 1987-89 tour, with just a few performances in 1994. In addition to the CD single, there were regular and pink vinyl 7" copies, and two 12" versions, one in a poster bag. All were backed by 'Terminal Frost', while the 12" and CD formats also had the live recording of 'The Dogs Of War' from Atlanta.

ON THE TURNING AWAY
(GILMOUR/MOORE)

When this song opens like a traditional ballad, with Gilmour singing almost *a cappella*, over a sparse keyboard drone, it is tempting to imagine him in an Aran sweater with his finger in his ear, performing an acoustic version to a bunch of bearded real ale drinkers in a back-room folk club. Sadly this is not to be, and *clichéd*, 'Wall'-like keyboards and unadventurous drums soon swell the song, before leading into a hearty rendition of Gilmour's rent-a-solo, which manages to save it from complete AOR tedium. The lyrics were again Moore's, with contributions from Gilmour.

When this was released as the second single from the album (EMI EM 34), it was backed by a live version of 'Run Like Hell'. As with 'One Slip', there were pink vinyl 7" and 12" poster bag singles, plus the usual plain 7", 12" and CD. Both the 12" and the CD versions had an additional, live, 'On The Turning Away', which, like 'Run Like Hell', was recorded in Atlanta.

YET ANOTHER MOVIE
(GILMOUR/LEONARD)

A lumbering song, lacking the dynamics which have given Pink Floyd the edge over so many of their imitators, it is again the guitar solo which provides the only excitement. Nevertheless, it was seen as one of the highlights of the album by Nick Mason, probably because of the attention that was paid to the drum sound, with Jim Keltner and percussionist Steve Forman playing in a very large studio. Instrumental extracts were used in *La Carrera Panamericana*.

The film dialogue in the background is "borrowed" from one of Marlon Brando's monologues in *On The Waterfront* and from *Casablanca* (Bogart's "You've got to listen... " at 5'24", through to Ingrid Bergman's "What have I done?").

ROUND AND AROUND
(GILMOUR)

An instrumental coda to 'Yet Another Movie', with which it was indexed as one track on CD. An unreleased five minute version is known to exist.

A NEW MACHINE PART 1
(GILMOUR)

Possibly the worst thing ever recorded by Pink Floyd, at least since 1970, with Gilmour's almost spoken lyrics pumped through a Vocoder and supported only by the weediest of keyboard tracks.

Gilmour has insisted that the title bears no relation to 'Welcome To The Machine'.

TERMINAL FROST
(GILMOUR)

A mood piece, ripe with guitar frills from start to finish, overlaid with sax and keyboards and restrained vocalese, to which Gilmour at one time considered adding vocals.

The CD single 'Learning To Fly' included, as a teaser track, 'Terminal Frost (DYOL version)', where DYOL stood for "Do Your Own Lead", parts of the lead guitar track allegedly having been mixed out in order to allow budding Gilmours to play along on their own guitar/tennis racquet/hairbrush, although there seems to be no appreciable difference.

A NEW MACHINE PART 2
(GILMOUR)

As the title implies, a continuation of 'Part 1'. Both 'A New Machine' and 'Terminal Frost' were written a couple of years before work started on the album.

SORROW
(GILMOUR)

Thought by many to be about Waters, a supposition which Gilmour has denied, pointing out that his inspiration for the lyrics was a poem, although he says he cannot remember which. For the first time in his career, Gilmour wrote the words before the tune. His line "of promises broken" was another contender for the album title. This was another of the songs whose tune was used in *La Carrera Panamericana*.

The impressive guitar sound was achieved by the clever, if expensive, trick of having Gilmour play through a concert PA in the L.A. Sports Arena, then recording the result. Gilmour claims the guitar solo was recorded first take, with no subsequent attempt to better it being considered necessary. Short backwards passages can be heard at 4'44" and 4'52".

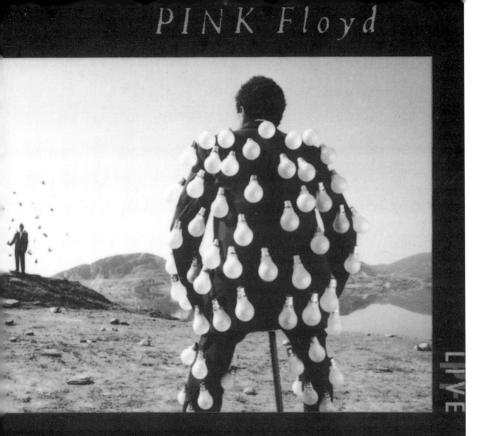

delicate sound of thunder

EMI CDS 7914802, released: November 22 1988

UK Chart: No. 11; US Chart: No. 11
Video: PMI MVN 9911863, released June 5 1989

In September 1987, the new Pink Floyd began what was intended to be a short tour of American arenas. In the end, demand for tickets was so great that the tour eventually ran to 200 dates over a three year period, also reaching Australia, New Zealand, Russia and Europe. For the tour, the three man Floyd were augmented by Guy Pratt (bass), Jon Carin (keyboards), Gary Wallis (drums), Tim Renwick (a Cambridge veteran and long-time friend of Gilmour's, guitar) and Scott Page (sax and occasional guitar). There were also a number of female backing vocalists, who came and went as the tour progressed. Initially, these were Margaret Taylor and Rachel Fury. When the Atlanta, Georgia concert of November 1987 was filmed for an abortive video and record (some tracks were used as single B-sides, and the show was scheduled, but never shown, by Irish television), three other vocalists, including Durga McBroom, were brought in, as she put it "to add colour". McBroom impressed sufficiently to be asked to remain in the band. (Taylor was replaced by Durga's sister, Lorelei, on the 1989 leg of the tour, which promoted this live album).

In August 1988, at New York's Nassau Coliseum, Pink Floyd recorded and filmed five shows for this two CD set, produced by David Gilmour, and a video, directed by Wayne Isham. The latter features additional footage shot at their historic gig outside the Palace of Versailles and is also available on laserdisc and VideoCD. There are reports that the band spent an entire afternoon taping one track in an otherwise empty Coliseum, repeating it some eight times until they got the take they wanted.

The film is hampered by Isham's dreamy style – lots of slow-motion, soft focus, long cross-fades – distracting the viewer from the visual spectacle that is a Pink Floyd concert. They may suit a short promo video, but after fifteen minutes become incredibly wearing. The Isham-directed televised concert performed at Venice has the same problem, but much less so. Even worse is the blue fog amidst which most of the concert seems to take place, giving no hint that the concerts were, in reality, very colourful affairs.

A possible reason for the abandonment of the Atlanta recordings arose when Gilmour admitted that, at the beginning of the tour, Wallis was playing all the drums and Carin the keyboards. Not until later did Gilmour consider that Mason and Wright had returned to being functioning musicians.

The sleeve was another Thorgerson design, the light-bulb covered man representing the visual spectacle of a Floyd show, the birds' flapping wings the sound.

One of the tour's T-shirt slogans, "Pink Floyd – First In Space" seemed unexpectedly prophetic when, four days after the album's release cosmonauts took a tape of 'Delicate...', and a Walkman-style player, with them to the Mir space station. Gilmour and Mason attended the launch of the Salyut rocket at the Soviet's Baikonur Cosmodrome, in Kazakhstan, previously the launch site for Sputnik and Uri Gagarin.

It is noticeable that every single track on the record, except the new material, includes Waters' name in the composers' credits.

Pink Floyd played only one concert in 1990, at Knebworth Park, alongside Robert Plant, Genesis, Eric Clapton, Paul McCartney and others. The festival was broadcast on BBC Radio One and screened on TV around the world, except in the UK, where only highlights were screened. It was also recorded, for 'Knebworth – The Album' (Polydor 843 921-2) and a set of three videos, *Knebworth – The Event*. Pink Floyd are only on Volume 3 (Castle Music Pictures CMP 6008). They contribute 'Comfortably Numb' to the album, 'Shine On You Crazy Diamond' to the video and 'Run Like Hell' to both. The line-up included Candy Dulfer, replacing Scott Page on saxophone and backing vocalists Sam Brown, her mother Vicki and Durga McBroom, plus the now familiar collection of backing musicians. Clare Torry made a guest appearance to reprise her vocal on 'Great Gig...' and Michael Kamen played on keyboards on 'Comfortably Numb'.

SHINE ON YOU CRAZY DIAMOND

To open all but the first few dates on the two hundred show tour, Pink Floyd chose 'Shine On... Parts 1-5'; a fine beginning, but unfortunately marred by a truly awful sax interjection, sadly typical of Scott Page's work on the tour. Video viewers are spared this, however, as only 'Part 1', Gilmour's guitar introduction, is shown.

The rest of the first CD is taken up with material from 'Momentary Lapse...'.

SIGNS OF LIFE
(on the video version only)
Although musically unspectacular, viewers do get the chance to see some of the special footage shot for the tour, although it would have been preferable if this had been spliced in directly, instead of filmed from the on-stage screen.

LEARNING TO FLY

Apart from some ad-libbed guitar and some inconsequential timpani during the last minute, this is little different from the album version. Gilmour regularly allowed Renwick to play much of the lead parts, opting to handle rhythm guitar while he sang.

Although the back-projected film is glimpsed from time to time, fans were disappointed that it was not included in full, feeling that its point was lost.

YET ANOTHER MOVIE
(omitted from the video version)
Despite some over-heavy echo on Gilmour's vocals, this too is close to the album version, film dialogue and all.

The visual highlight of the track's concert presentation was Mason and Wallis' use of colour-shifting neon drumsticks, which were even more impressive from a distance, with the stage lights dimmed. Since the track is not on the video, Isham shifted them to footage of 'Time', but their original location is given away by the otherwise inexplicable cheer about half a minute into this track.

ROUND AND AROUND
(omitted from the video version)
Now indexed separately from 'Yet Another Movie', at thirty-four seconds this was once the shortest track released in the history of Pink Floyd, until the indexing of 'The Show Must Go On', on the remastered 'Wall' CD, stole its thunder.

SORROW
Only marginally longer than the studio version, and not very different from it.

THE DOGS OF WAR
Gilmour appears briefly in the Storm Thorgerson directed film, which was back-projected during the concert. Again, extra guitar livens the track up slightly.

ON THE TURNING AWAY
Differs from the 'Momentary Lapse...' version only by virtue of a lengthened keyboard intro and an extended guitar coda.

ONE OF THESE DAYS
Disc two opens where the second, "oldies" set

of the concert began, and is a greatest hits selection unblemished by 'Momentary Lapse...' material. The menace of 'One Of These Days' was the ideal time to fly Pink Floyd's new pig, which had added gonads, to avoid copyright problems over Roger Waters' pig, a sow. Even so, the video tetchily credits "Original Pig Concept by R. Waters". Although the pig is seen in the video, it never appears clearly enough to be properly appreciated.

TIME
Rick Wright's lead vocals are pleasingly confident, after so long out of the saddle.

The video shows some of the original animated film, by Ian Eames, to good effect, but the neon drumsticks are borrowed from 'Yet Another Movie'.

ON THE RUN
(on the video version only)
New film, featuring the same character from 'Signs Of Life', is seen behind the band, emphasising the sense of paranoia.

Not quite so clear is the bed which flew (down a wire) from the upper rear of the auditorium to crash in flames on the stage. At other

concerts, this was replaced by a winged creature, nicknamed "Icarus" by fans, which flew during 'Learning To Fly'.

THE GREAT GIG IN THE SKY
(on the video version only)
Good though they are, the three vocalists can't match the power of Torry's original. The firework footage is from the Versailles gig.

WISH YOU WERE HERE
Gilmour and Renwick duet on acoustic guitar.

US AND THEM
(omitted from the vinyl version)
More of the back-projected film is used here than on other numbers, although it is galling to see some parts of it only in the corner of the screen.

MONEY
(omitted from the cassette and video versions)
Although this starts as a straightforward rendition, it is extended to almost ten minutes by a series of solos taken by each of the musicians and vocalists in turn. Purists were offended by the fact that this "jam" changed very little from night to night on the tour, with

Pratt's reggae riffing coming in for the strongest criticism.

ANOTHER BRICK IN THE WALL PART II
(omitted from the video version)
Complete with taped school-kid vocalists, this too had a radically reworked ending, with guitar and bass solos. The peculiar fade was more impressive in concert, when the children's contribution was panned around the venue using the band's legendary "Azimuth Co-Ordinator" – a joystick which could be used to alter the quad mix, varying the signal sent to each set of speakers.

COMFORTABLY NUMB
Although bassist Guy Pratt often handled Waters' vocal part, the video shows Jon Carin and Rick Wright sharing it.

With anyone else, the idea of a mirrorball would be a laughable cliché, but in Pink Floyd's hands it became a concert highlight. This might have something to do with the fact that the one which rose during Gilmour's extended guitar solo was absolutely huge and unfurled in mid-song, opening like a flower.

Sadly Isham's film barely captures this, one of the most memorable – and talked about – highlights of the show. Worse, the solo is edited to the point of butchery. Also, due to bad editing during the first guitar break, Gilmour can clearly be seen to rest his hand while his playing still emanates from the speakers.

ONE SLIP
(only on the video version)
Guy Pratt gets to show off his thumb-slap bass (whatever would Roger have said?) and Page plays an electric guitar.

RUN LIKE HELL
Almost invariably performed as the last encore, with Pratt again taking Waters' vocal lines, this and 'One Slip' always seemed to be an anticlimax after 'Comfortably Numb', both visually and aurally, despite the arsenal of fireworks with which it was concluded.

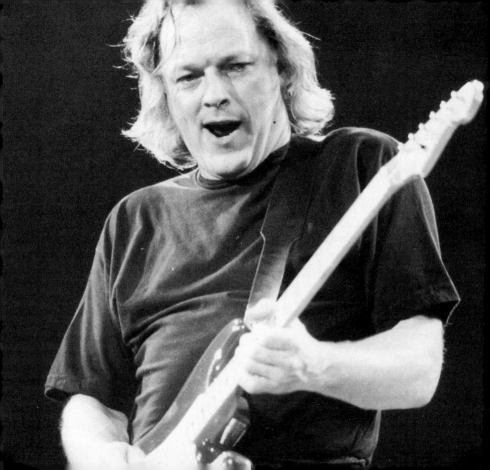

la carrera panamericana

Music Club Video MC 2134; previously available as: Picture Music International MVN 991 345 3, released: April 13 1992

Tracks: Run Like Hell; Pan Am Shuffle; Yet Another Movie; Sorrow; Signs Of Life; Country Theme; Mexico '78; Big Theme; Run Like Hell; One Slip; Small Theme; Pan Am Shuffle; Carrera Slow Blues.

In October 1991, David Gilmour and Nick Mason took part in a 2,500 mile motor race in Mexico, *La Carrera Panamericana*. They funded their involvement by accepting sponsorship and producing this documentary film, for which they provided an instrumental soundtrack.

The event recreated the original race, which was abandoned in 1954 after a spate of accidents. Gilmour and manager Steve O'Rourke drove one replica C-Type Jaguar, Mason and Valentine Lindsay (an employee of Ten Tenths, the company that manages Mason's extensive vehicle collection) drove another. Mason and Lindsay came eighth overall, but Gilmour and O'Rourke failed to finish after O'Rourke crashed their car, suffering a broken leg. Gilmour was lucky to escape with bruising.

The film, directed and produced by Ian McArthur, was premièred on BBC 2 television in December that year, but the commercially released video is slightly different. As well as snippets of 'Run Like Hell' and tracks from 'Momentary Lapse...', several new tunes were used, produced by David Gilmour. 'Pan Am Shuffle' and 'Carrera Slow Blues' were the first Gilmour/Mason/Wright compositions since 'Any Colour You Like'. The remaining new pieces were written by Gilmour and all were performed by the trio with the assistance of Jon Carin, Guy Pratt, Gary Wallis and Tim Renwick. Despite initial suggestions to the contrary, the new material did not reappear on 'The Division Bell'.

shine on

EMI 7 80557 2, released: November 9 1992

A lavishly-packaged box set including: 'A Saucerful Of Secrets'; 'Meddle'; 'Dark Side Of The Moon'; 'Wish You Were Here'; 'Animals'; 'The Wall' and 'A Momentary Lapse Of Reason'. All the albums were digitally remastered and came in a special set of black jewel cases which, when stood side-by-side, had the 'Dark Side...' prism on their spines. Also in the box were postcards, a book and a "bonus disc", compiling both sides of each of the band's first five singles, again, all digitally re-mastered.

While this provided many newly-converted CD buyers with an economical way to acquire seven of the Floyd's best-loved albums in one go, committed fans considered the band to have shot themselves in the foot. Although they could now obtain the early singles on CD, they had hoped for more rarities, in the form of unre-leased tracks, out-takes and live recordings, instead of just albums they already had. What they got instead was a collection of rain-forest threatening packaging and a furry (as opposed to glossy) book whose myriad inaccuracies and omissions were overshadowed by the fact that the final page ended in mid-sentence. Perhaps the mysterious sounds at the end of 'Dark Side...' had been added to drown out the cries of proof-readers being mercilessly flogged?

Unlike all other CD versions, 'Dark Side Of The Moon' indexes 'Speak To Me' and 'Breathe' as two tracks. On 'The Wall', the indexing errors on 'Young Lust' and 'One Of My Turns' were corrected. Of all the albums included, 'Animals' probably showed the greatest improvement, losing the layer of audio murk which had marred the first CD issue. On the other hand, having only recently been digitally recorded, 'Momentary Lapse...' needed no re-mastering.

In the jumbled up lettering on the CD labels can be discerned "the Big Bong Theory", once a contender for the box's title, but vetoed as "too drug inspired".

Although it has its own catalogue number (7 80572 2), 'The Pink Floyd Early Singles', as the digi-pack mounted disc was titled, is not officially available as a separate release, but has been bootlegged in a professionally-packaged jewel-case. It comprised:

ARNOLD LAYNE
(BARRETT)

Originally recorded at the Whitehead-funded demo sessions in January 1967, this was re-recorded in the following month, at Sound Techniques with the now-legendary producer Joe Boyd (the credit reads "produced by Joe Boyd for Blackhill Enterprises"), as the band's first single (Columbia DB 8156), reaching number 28 in the UK charts.

The song tells the tale of a clothes-stealing transvestite and was inspired by the theft of underwear from Waters and Barrett's mothers' female student lodgers. Such debauchery was not for pirate station Radio London, although the record was played by the BBC. The band, although irritated at the oversimplification of the issue, viewed this with some

disinterest, since they had not wanted the single released anyway, feeling that they had progressed from such simple pop melodies.

A promo film was shot, with Syd and the rest of the band messing around with a shop window dummy. Waters screened this during an on-stage "tea-break" during his 1987 concerts.

CANDY AND A CURRANT BUN
(BARRETT)

First recorded at the Whitehead session, the B-side of 'Arnold' was originally known as 'Let's Roll Another One', the lyrics blatantly describing the joys of soft drugs. EMI naturally balked at the idea of releasing such a ditty, and insisted both title and lyrics be changed, although the "tastes good..." lyric remained.

SEE EMILY PLAY
(BARRETT)

The next single, 'See Emily Play' (Columbia DB 8214), recorded at the same time as 'Piper...' preceded the album, although Norman Smith found it necessary to return to Sound Techniques to recapture the sound and spirit of 'Arnold Layne'. A visitor to the studio during the recording sessions was Barrett's friend from Cambridge, David Gilmour. 'Emily...' was promoted with three appearances on *Top Of The Pops*. Criminally, all three master tapes were erased by the BBC in the Eighties, when the storage space was needed for other programmes.

The song was written as 'Games For May', to mark a festival of the same name, held at the Queen Elizabeth Hall in London in May 1967. Indeed, the original title remains among the revised lyrics, although Barrett later claimed it was about a girl he saw in a wood "Up North", where he was sleeping after a concert. It achieved a few further live performances, chiefly to appease pop fans who went to se the band on the strength of the single's position at No. 6 in the UK chart, and were bewildered by the more typical instrumental jams.

A very limited number of promo copies, now much sought-after by collectors, were issued in picture sleeves, depicting a child-like drawing of a train by Barrett. His artwork was also used in press adverts for the disc.

A promo film, believed to have been shot by a Belgian TV station, has the Gilmour-era band messing about in a park and making no

attempt to mime while the studio recording plays. The film is available on a various-artist video compilation, 'Rock'n'Roll Years 1967' (Video Collection VC 4058)

SCARECROW
(BARRETT)

'Emily's B-side was exactly the same as the version which would appear on 'Piper...'. It was the subject of an early – and suitably bizarre – promo film, made for a Pathé newsreel, giving the young Floyds an excuse for much cavorting and hamming.

APPLES AND ORANGES
(BARRETT)

Barrett's final single for the band (Columbia DB 8310) was recorded in only two sessions, Waters claiming that Smith's botched production had spoiled a perfectly good song. Barrett claimed his inspiration was a girl he had seen while shopping.

It was recorded for the BBC in October 1967 and mimed by the band for their first US TV appearance, on the *Dick Clarke Bandstand,* with Barrett especially seeming unwilling to co-operate. A 1968 promo video has Waters miming the vocals and Gilmour the guitar.

Like 'Emily...', promo copies came in a much-sought-after picture sleeve, but with a weak design in which the band had no hand.

PAINTBOX
(WRIGHT)

The B-side of 'Apples And Oranges' was sung by its composer. The lyrics "Sitting in a club with so many fools/Playing to the rules/Trying to impress, but feeling rather empty" give a clear indication of how Wright, and indeed the whole band, felt when asked to perform their pop hits instead of their preferred psychedelic improvisations.

IT WOULD BE SO NICE
(WRIGHT)

The first post-Syd single, (Columbia DB 8410), was recorded at around the time the album was being completed. Sung by Wright, this was his only Floyd composition released as a single A-side, and disappeared without trace, probably because the promising, powerful intro soon descended into a novelty-song style verse, rendered listenable only by the harmonies on the chorus. The band themselves soon expressed their dislike of the song.

An original reference to London's *Evening Standard* newspaper had to be changed to the fictitious "Daily Standard" after complaints from the publisher. The latter version is heard here, and on all other known compilations.

JULIA DREAM
(WATERS)

'It Would Be So Nice' was backed by Gilmour's vocal début for the band, in a style very similar to his singing on 'Fat Old Sun'. Although not a concert number, it was recorded for the BBC in June 1968.

The song is an early example of Waters writing about paranoia ("Will the following footsteps catch me... Am I really dying?") and there is much debate over whether Waters' whispered words in the final moments are "Syd", "Save Me" or, as seems more likely, something else entirely.

POINT ME AT THE SKY
(WATERS/GILMOUR)

Six months after the 'Saucerful...' album, Pink Floyd released their last single for 11 years, (Columbia DB 8511). Although never performed live, a promo film was made for 'Point Me...', featuring the band dressed in Bigglesstyle flying suits and cavorting with a bi-plane. The song was also filmed for *Tous En Scène* and recorded, with a minor lyric change, for the band's December 1968 BBC session. On record, Gilmour handles lead vocals, with Wright joining in and Waters singing the lyrics about "People pushing on my side..."

Lyrically, this is the strongest of the five early singles, a seemingly simple tale of an intrepid aviator soon giving way to a warning about the dangers of an overcrowded planet, perhaps an early recognition of the environmental concerns now so prevalent among successful pop stars.

CAREFUL WITH THAT AXE, EUGENE
(WATERS/WRIGHT/GILMOUR/MASON)

The only single-side drawn from the band's live set, this brooding, menacing instrumental first appeared, in 1968, as 'Murderistic Woman', (recorded for the June '68 BBC session), later being called 'Keep Smiling People'. It also made appearances under the moniker 'Beset By Creatures Of The Deep', part of 'The Journey'. It was recorded again in May '69, under its more familiar title, for the BBC and, at around the same time, for 'Ummagumma'. Another live version, from 1971, can be seen and heard in the 'Superstars In Concert' video (Telstar TVE 1003), while a different performance is in *Live At Pompeii*. Only on versions with this name is the title pronounced by Waters before the track's high-point, his scream. Another studio version, 'Come In No. 51, Your Time Is Up', was used in the film *Zabriskie Point*.

The piece had also been used among the 15 minutes of instrumental music recorded in 1968 by the band for another film soundtrack, *The Committee*, which was never fully released, although it was shown to the press. A soundtrack album was proposed at one time. Perhaps, like *Tonite Let's All Make Love In London*, the film and music master tapes are gathering dust somewhere, waiting for some keen entrepreneur to sort out contractual hassles and release them to eager fans.

Dropped from the live set in October 1973, 'Axe' was resurrected for an unexpected, one-off concert encore in Oakland, California in May 1977.

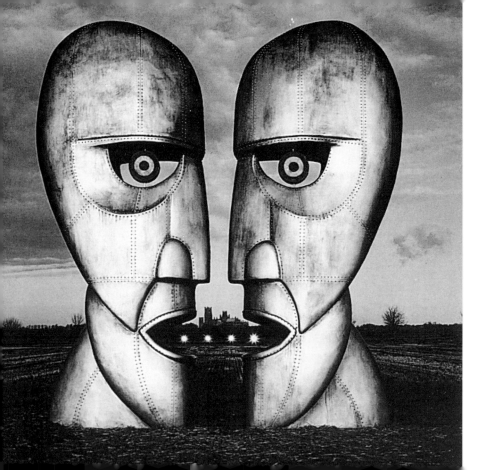

the division bell

EMI 8 28984 2, released March 30 1994

UK Chart: No. 1; US Chart: No. 1

Released on the same day that Pink Floyd opened their 1994 tour, the first thing most buyers noticed was that each format boasted a subtly different, but similar sleeve, showing two giant heads, designed and photographed by Storm Thorgerson with Ely Cathedral in the background. In each case, the heads were shot under different lighting conditions and were made from different materials. Further variants were found in the tour programme and song book, and on overseas editions.

Despite claims that the album had been written during jamming sessions involving the three remaining members of Pink Floyd, joined by Guy Pratt on bass, there were no writing credits for Mason or Pratt. Many of the lyrics were co-written by Gilmour and his girlfriend, later wife, former Sunday Times writer Polly Samson. Another helper was Nick Laird-Clowes, formerly leader of The Dream Academy, whose first and third albums Gilmour produced.

Although far from a Floydian concept album, 'The Division Bell' has a general theme of communication gone wrong. The title is taken from the bell which is rung in the House Of Commons to warn MPs that a vote, or division, is about to take place. Author Douglas Adams named the album. He explained: "Dave Gilmour asked me to fiddle around some of the album lyrics, which I did, though I don't think he used any of my suggestions in the end. The only suggestion of mine that I know was used was that the album should be called 'The Division Bell'. I didn't think up the title, of course. I merely pointed out that the phrase was lying there in one of the song lyrics and would make a great title. Dave was a bit preoccupied about the title problem – they had to have the title by the following morning, and no one could decide what it should be. I said 'OK, I'll give you a title, but it'll cost you a £5,000 contribution to the Environmental Investigation Agency!' Dave said 'Well, tell me what your title is and we'll see'. So I suggested 'The Division Bell' and Dave said 'Hmmm, well, seems to work. Sort of fits the cover art as well. Yeah, OK'."

The album was jointly produced by Gilmour and Bob Ezrin. An army of session musicians was again called upon to contribute, including many from the previous tours: Jon Carin, Guy Pratt, Gary Wallis and Tim Renwick. Ezrin added keyboard and percussion and Michael Kamen was again responsible for orchestration. A surprising, and welcome, return to the fold was made by saxophonist Dick Parry. Durga McBroom, fresh from success with her own band Blue Pearl, returned on backing vocals, alongside another chart star, Sam Brown. Other backing vocals were added by Carol Kenyon, Jackie Sheridan and Rebecca Leigh-White.

Carin, Pratt, Wallis, Renwick, Parry, McBroom and Brown also joined Gilmour, Mason and Wright (a full member of the band once again), plus a third vocalist, Claudia Fontaine, for a tour of America and Europe.

CLUSTER ONE
(WRIGHT/GILMOUR)

The album's instrumental introduction was also used in the lengthy intro tape which heralded the band's arrival on stage in concert. Bluesy guitar is predominant, over some echoey piano and drums that do not come in until near the end.

WHAT DO YOU WANT FROM ME
(MUSIC: GILMOUR/WRIGHT.
LYRICS: GILMOUR/SAMSON)

Smothered with guitar straight from 'Wish You Were Here', and displaying excellent use of the backing vocalists, this apparent dig at Pink Floyd fans actually takes its title from something shouted during a row between Gilmour and Samson, though who said it to whom is not known!

POLES APART
(MUSIC: GILMOUR.
LYRICS: GILMOUR/SAMSON/LAIRD-CLOWES)

Samson has stated categorically that the first verse of this team effort is about Barrett, the second about Waters. Gilmour's vocal delivery harks back to his 1984 solo album 'About Face' and is not a style he has previously employed with Pink Floyd. The Hammond organ riff during the middle-eight is blissful, but the point of the sequence preceding the third verse is unclear. Although this was performed live, it was never heard more than a handful of times.

MAROONED
(GILMOUR/WRIGHT)

A guitar-based instrumental, in places similar to the end of 'Comfortably Numb'. Performed live for the first time halfway through the European leg of the 1994 tour, in Norway, where the back-projected accompaniment, film of whales at sea, may have been a dig at the host country's continued whaling activity.

A GREAT DAY FOR FREEDOM
(MUSIC: GILMOUR.
LYRICS: GILMOUR/SAMSON)

Like 'Atom Heart Mother', the title is a newspaper headline (clearly illustrated in the album's packaging), but its tale of the collapse of the Berlin Wall was covered much more effectively on Roy Harper's 'Berliners', to which Gilmour had contributed guitar in 1990.

The music is also weak, though whether this or the need for Gilmour to repeatedly deny that it alludes to the split with Waters (and his Berlin performance of 1990) explain its infrequent live outings is unknown.

WEARING THE INSIDE OUT
(MUSIC: WRIGHT. LYRICS: MOORE)

Opening with laid-back sax from Parry, Wright's first attempt at writing music for the band unaided since 'Wish You Were Here' still relied on outside talent for the lyrics, in the guise of 'Momentary Lapse...' veteran Anthony Moore. Nevertheless, they could be describing Wright's post-'Wall' estrangement from the band in his own words. It was a surprise to hear Rick Wright record a vocal lead after so many years in the wilderness, but this treat was to be denied to live audiences as no performances are known to have been made.

Gilmour handles vocals on a couple of the verses before closing with one of the album's more tasteful guitar solos.

Two of the verses are sung by the backing singers simultaneously with Wright's vocals.

TAKE IT BACK
(MUSIC: GILMOUR/EZRIN.
LYRICS: GILMOUR/SAMSON/LAIRD-CLOWES)

The music's resemblance to U2, especially the Edge's choppy guitar, attracted both comment and criticism, although, to be fair, The Edge's playing on 'Silver And Gold' and 'Bullet The Blue Sky' owes a great debt to mid-Seventies Floyd.

When this was released as the first single from the album (EMI 8 81278 7), with a video directed by Marc Brickman, better known as Pink Floyd's lighting director, fans received another surprise: the B-side was a live recording, from the tour's opening show, of 'Astronomy Domine'!

COMING BACK TO LIFE
(GILMOUR)

The only song on the album where Gilmour managed to write all the lyrics unaided (although the paucity of live performances suggests that he is not especially proud of them) opens with a bluesy guitar passage, followed by his breathy vocals. A simple rhythm develops as the second verse starts, but the guitar solo is restrained and the track never really goes anywhere.

KEEP TALKING
(MUSIC: GILMOUR/WRIGHT.
LYRICS: GILMOUR/SAMSON)

The opening monologue, more familiar as a British Telecom advert, is the words and voice of physicist Stephen Hawking, author of the famous and unfathomable *A Brief History Of Time*, who can communicate only via a speech-synthesising computer owing to motor-neurone disease.

Gilmour's use of Vocoder is very reminiscent of 'Pigs (Three Different Ones)', although some of his guitar is more typical of 'The Wall' and 'The Final Cut'.

To mark their record-breaking fourteen nights at London's Earls Court in October 1994, a "radio edit" of the track appeared on a double A-side single with 'High Hopes'.

LOST FOR WORDS
(MUSIC: GILMOUR.
LYRICS: GILMOUR/SAMSON)

Gilmour has denied that the lyrics – and particularly the final verse – refer to his former colleague, Roger Waters, despite fans' and critics' assumptions to the contrary. This may explain why it graced only a few 1994 concerts.

The opening footsteps, rattling chain and closing gate, plus the boxing announcement after the third verse, are among the last vestiges of the *musique concrète* which has been a trademark of the band's work for so many years.

HIGH HOPES
(MUSIC: GILMOUR
LYRICS: GILMOUR/SAMSON)

Gilmour has admitted that this, the first thing he wrote for the album, is more personal than his usual style, and that it set the tone for the rest of the album. Its middle-eight Spanish guitar and marching drums, with orchestral backing, sound like leftovers from 'The Wall'.

The bell which bookends the track is not the parliamentary Division Bell, but may be intended to represent one at a Cambridge College, or those of Ely Cathedral, both of which feature in Storm Thorgerson's promo video for the song, as does the Gilmour family's former home in Cambridge.

A "radio edit" of 'High Hopes' became the album's second single (EMI 8 81773 2) where, although presented as a double A-side with 'Keep Talking', it appeared to be the lead track: not only were its lyrics reproduced on the sleeve, but the front cover was from its promotional video, as were the images on the seven "film cards" included in a limited edition package. The cards were also included with a 12" coloured, etched vinyl edition. The extra track in all cases was a live version of 'One Of These Days'.

The last thing heard on the album – it's very quiet – is a recording of Samson's son Charlie hanging up the telephone on Floyd manager Steve O'Rourke, emphasising the album's theme of poor communications. This is the band's witty response to O'Rourke's constant requests to be allowed to play a few notes on a Floyd album.

overseas compilations

A few of the many compilations released around the globe are of special interest because they offer fans the chance to obtain rare recordings without paying over the odds for original singles. Those on CD also offer, of course, better quality. The sooner Pink Floyd allow EMI to collect these, and other, rare tracks and release them properly, the happier fans will be.

MASTERS OF ROCK VOL. 1
HARVEST 1 C 054-04 299,
RELEASED: 1974

Tracks: *Chapter 24; Mathilda Mother (sic); Arnold Layne; Candy And A Currant Bun; Scarecrow; Apples And Oranges; It Would Be So Nice; Paint Box; Julia Dream; See Emily Play.*

A now-deleted vinyl-only release, originally issued in 1970 as 'The Best of Pink Floyd',

using as its cover the group portrait from 'Meddle'. This, more common, version was later released in Germany, Italy and nearby territories (and widely imported into the UK), in a generic sleeve with gold graphics. Both editions are sought after because of the inclusion of some early singles which have never been reissued outside the 'Shine On' box set. Subsequent volumes in the series were by other bands.

WORKS

CAPITOL CDP 7 46478 2; ORIGINALLY
CAPITOL ST 12276, RELEASED: CIRCA 1983

Tracks: One Of These Days; Arnold Layne; Fearless; Brain Damage/ Eclipse; Set The Controls For The Heart Of The Sun; See Emily Play; Several Species Of Small Furry Animals Gathered Together In A Cave And Grooving With A Pict; Free Four; Embryo.

Released only in the US, but widely available in the UK as an import, this "hits" compilation only goes up to 'Dark Side...', after which Pink Floyd changed their Stateside label to Columbia. It is notable for the re-emergence of 'Embryo' and the inclusion of some different mixes, especially 'Brain Damage' and 'Eclipse', which are taken from quadrophonic masters.

A CD FULL OF SECRETS

WESTWOOD ONE VOL. 10,
RELEASED: CIRCA 1992

Tracks: Candy And A Currant Bun; See Emily Play; Flaming (US single version); Apples And Oranges; Paintbox; It Would Be So Nice; Julia Dream; Point Me At The Sky; Heartbeat, Pigmeat; Crumbling Land; Come In Number 51, Your Time Is Up; Biding My Time; Money (1981 dance version); When The Tigers Broke Free; Not Now John (obscured version); Terminal Frost (DYOL mix); Run Like Hell (live version).

Released for radio use only, in the US, and useful not only because of its relatively wide availability, but also for including most of the non-album single sides (except 'Arnold Layne', the longer version of 'The Hero's Return' and some live cuts), notably the only CD versions of the US single mix of 'Flaming' and the "polite", single version of 'Not Now John'. It has also been pirated, by a label claiming to be based in Luxembourg.

The 'dance' version of 'Money' is the version from 'Great Dance Songs'. The live 'Run Like Hell' is from the 'On The Turning Away' single.

The Madcap Laughs / Barrett: Syd Barrett

Opel: Syd Barrett

Radio KAOS: Roger Waters

The Wall - Live In Berlin: Roger Waters

solo recordings

L ike their colleagues in bands of similar stature, the members and former members of Pink Floyd have recorded solo albums. In the case of David Gilmour, Nick Mason and Rick Wright, these were either ways of passing the time (and tax exile) between band projects, or extra-curricular dalliances that allowed them to release music incompatible with "The Pink Floyd Sound". However, the solo projects of Syd Barrett (particularly given the involvement of his former band-mates) and, latterly, Roger Waters, give us glimpses of the alternative Pink Floyds which may have existed had fate had different tricks to play.

syd barrett

THE MADCAP LAUGHS

HARVEST 8 28906 2;
ORIGINALLY HARVEST SHVL 765;
PREVIOUSLY HARVEST CDP 7 46607 2,
RELEASED: JANUARY 1970

Tracks: Terrapin; No Good Trying; Love You; No Man's Land; Dark Globe; Here I Go; Octopus; Golden Hair; Long Gone;.She Took A Long Cold Look; Feel; If It's In You; Late Night
Bonus Tracks: Octopus (Takes 1 & 2); It's No Good Trying (Take 5); Love You (Take 1); Love You (Take 3); She Took A Long Cold Look At Me (Take 4); Golden Hair (Take 5)

Variously produced by Dave Gilmour and Roger Waters, Malcolm Jones, Dave Gilmour and Syd Barrett and Peter Jenner. Only the most recent CD contained the bonus tracks.

'Golden Hair' is a poem by James Joyce, set to music by Barrett, and was the B-side of Barrett's only single, 'Octopus' (Harvest HAR 5009).

BARRETT

HARVEST 8 28907 2;
ORIGINALLY HARVEST SHSP 4007;
PREVIOUSLY HARVEST CDP 7 466606 2,
RELEASED: NOVEMBER 1970

Tracks: Baby Lemonade; Love Song; Dominoes; It Is Obvious; Rats; Maisie; Gigolo Aunt; Waving My Arms In The Air/ I Never Lied To You; Wined And Dined; Wolfpack; Effervescing Elephant
Bonus Tracks: Baby Lemonade (Take 1); Waving My Arms In The Air (Take 1); I Never Lied To You (Take 1); Love Song (Take 1); Dominoes (Take 1); Dominoes (Take 2); It Is Obvious (Take 2)

Produced by Dave Gilmour. Only the most recent CD contained the bonus tracks, but earlier releases credit Richard Wright as co-producer. The first two Barrett solo albums were available, on vinyl only, as the double album 'Syd Barrett' (Harvest SHDW404).

THE PEEL SESSION
STRANGE FRUIT SFPSCD 043,
RELEASED: FEBRUARY 1988

Tracks: Terrapin; Gigolo Aunt; Effervescing Elephant; Two Of A Kind; Baby Lemonade

Recorded for the BBC Radio 1's *Top Gear* show on May 18, 1970 (DJ John Peel), with Jerry Shirley (drums) and David Gilmour (bass). Produced by John Walters. Although credited to Syd, many fans argue that 'Two Of A Kind' is a Rick Wright composition. Barrett also recorded three songs, 'Baby Lemonade'' 'Domino' and 'Love Song', for the BBC in March 1971, but sadly the master tape is missing from the BBC archives.

OPEL
HARVEST 8 28908 2;
PREVIOUSLY HARVEST CDP 7 91206 2,
RELEASED: OCTOBER 17 1988

Tracks: Opel; Clowns & Jugglers (Octopus); Rats; Golden Hair; Dolly Rocker; Word Song; Wined & Dined; Swan Lee (Silas Lang); Birdie Hop; Let's Split; Lanky (Part 1); Wouldn't You Miss Me (Dark Globe); Milky Way; Golden Hair (Instrumental) Bonus Tracks: Gigolo Aunt (Take 9); It Is Obvious (Take 3); It Is Obvious (Take 5); Clowns & Jugglers (Take 1); Late Night (Take 2); Effervescing Elephant (Take 2)

Compilation of demos, alternate takes and unreleased material from the first two albums, with various producers. Only the most recent CD contained the bonus tracks.

CRAZY DIAMOND - THE COMPLETE SYD BARRETT
HARVEST CDS 7 81412 2,
RELEASED: APRIL 26 1993

This three CD box set includes 'The Madcap Laughs', 'Barrett' and 'Opel', each with bonus tracks, plus a 24 page booklet. The extended discs were later released individually, as listed above.

david gilmour

UNTITLED
(as Jokers Wild)
(UNNUMBERED PRIVATE PRESSING, RELEASED: CIRCA 1965)

Tracks: Why Do Fools Fall In Love; Walk Like A Man; Don't Ask Me (What I Say); Big Girls Don't Cry; Beautiful Delilah

Prior to joining Pink Floyd, David Gilmour cut a five track, one-sided album with his band Jokers Wild. Only 40 or 50 copies were pressed, for family and friends. All the songs are soul standards, and two, 'Don't Ask Me' and 'Why Do Fools Fall In Love', were used on a 7" single, which had an equally limited run. In 1994, a copy sold for over £800, but readers can avoid the expense by visiting the National Sound Archive in London, where a tape-recording of the album can be heard by personal callers who quote reference "C-625/1".

DAVID GILMOUR
HARVEST SHVL 817 (UK VINYL); COLUMBIA CK 35388 (USA CD), RELEASED: MAY 25 1978

Tracks: Mihalis; There's No Way Out Of Here; Cry From The Street; So Far Away; Short And Sweet; Raise My Rent; No Way; Definitely; I Can't Breathe Anymore

In 1978, while Waters prepared demos of 'The Wall' and 'Pros And Cons Of Hitch Hiking', Gilmour worked on his first proper solo album with Rick Wills and Willie Wilson, respectively the bassist and drummer he had toured France with before joining Pink Floyd. The trio returned to France for the recording sessions, produced by David Gilmour, which took place at Superbear Studios.

The album's only single, an edit of 'There's No Way Out Of Here', originally appeared on Unicorn's 'Too Many Crooks' album as 'No Way Out Of Here'. 'Short And Sweet' was written with Roy Harper for his 'Unknown Soldier' LP, on which Gilmour played.

ABOUT FACE
HARVEST CDP 7 46031 2;
ORIGINALLY HARVEST SHSP 24-0079-1,
RELEASED: MARCH 5 1984

Tracks: Until We Sleep; Murder; Love On The Air; Blue Light; Out Of The Blue; All Lovers Are Deranged; You Know I'm Right; Cruise; Let's Get Metaphysical; Near The End

'About Face', produced by Bob Ezrin and Gilmour, was the latter's response to the hiatus in Pink Floyd work after 'The Final Cut'. Although Pete Townshend contributed the lyrics of 'Love On The Air' and 'All Lovers Are Deranged', Gilmour wrote everything else and his songs are certainly up to scratch, making it hard to understand why he has needed so much help on subsequent Floyd albums. He assembled a band for a seventy-odd date tour of Europe and America, but the audiences were not of Pink Floyd proportions.

'Blue Light' was issued as a 7" and 12" single, both backed by 'Cruise' (Harvest HAR 5226). In the USA, there was another 12", with vocal and instrumental remixes by François Kevorkian and Frank Filipetti (Columbia 44-04983). This was only released in the UK as a DJ promo (DG1).

The follow-up, 'Love On The Air'/ 'Let's Get Metaphysical' was put out in 7" and picture disc formats, the latter in the outline of a valve radio, backed with a picture of David Gilmour (HAR 5229).

nick mason

FICTITIOUS SPORTS
HARVEST SHSP 4116 (UK VINYL);
SONY WK75070 (USA CD),
RELEASED: MAY 1981

Tracks: Can't Get My Motor To Start; I Was Wrong; Siam; Hot River; Boo To You Too; Do Ya?; Wervin'; I'm A Mineralist

Mason's first solo effort, released in 1981, was a collaboration with jazz artist Carla Bley. All compositions are by Bley, who co-produced the album with Mason, using her band and her "Grog Kill" studio in New York. The album certainly has much more in common with her work than Pink Floyd, even if 'Hot River' is a superb Floyd pastiche, with Gilmour's guitar mimicked by Chris Spedding and vocals by Robert Wyatt.

PROFILES
(with Rick Fenn)
HARVEST MAF 1 (UK VINYL);
SONY A40142 (USA CD),
RELEASED: AUGUST 19 1985

Tracks: Malta; Lie For A Lie; Rhoda; Profiles Parts 1 & 2; Israel; And The Address; Mumbo Jumbo; Zip Code; Black Ice; At The End Of The Day; Profiles Part 3

Profiles is a joint project with Rick Fenn, formerly guitarist for 10CC and Mike Oldfield's band. Mason and Fenn jointly wrote the music and produced the album at their studios, Britannia Row and The Basement respectively. The lyrics to the album's only songs, 'Lie For A Lie' and 'Israel', are by Danny Peyronel, who also sang on the latter, the only track written without Mason.

Additional contributions came from Mel Collins (sax), Craig Pruess (emulator bass on Malta), Danny Peyronel (vocals on Israel) and Fenn's five-year-old daughter Aja (keyboard intro on Malta). 'Lie For A Lie', with vocals by Maggie Reilly and David Gilmour, was released as a single, backed by 'And The

Address' (Harvest HAR 5238).

The title track is from the soundtrack to a biographical film about Mason, "Life Could Be A Dream", which was only ever given a very limited release. It also included a cover of the Crew Cuts' 'Sh'boom', with 10CC's Eric Stewart on vocals, which is sadly not heard on the album.

roger
waters

MUSIC FROM THE BODY
(with Ron Geesin)

HARVEST CDP 7 92548 2;
ORIGINALLY HARVEST SHSP 4008,
RELEASED: CIRCA 1970
WARNER BROTHERS PES 38196 (VIDEO)

Tracks: Our Song (Waters/ Geesin); Sea Shell And Stone (Waters); Red Stuff Writhe; A Gentle Breeze Blew Through Life; Lick Your Partners; Bridge Passage For Three Plastic Teeth; Chain Of Life (Waters); The Womb Bit (Waters/ Geesin); Embryo Thought; March Past Of The Embryos; More Than Seven Dwarfs In Penis-Land; Dance Of The Red Corpuscles; Body Transport (Waters/ Geesin); Hand Dance - Full Evening Dress; Breathe (Waters); Old Folks Ascension; Bedtime-Dream-Clime; Piddle In Perspex; Embryonic Womb-Walk; Mrs. Throat Goes Walking; Sea Shell And Soft Stone (Waters/ Geesin); Give Birth To A Smile (Waters)

The Body was an innovative (for its time) medical documentary, directed by Roy Battersby, in which Waters narrated one scene. Music, written by Geesin unless shown, from the film was re-recorded for the "soundtrack" album, produced by the two musicians.

On 'Give Birth To A Smile', Waters is joined by Gilmour, Wright and Mason. Although Waters and Geesin are given equal credit for this album, it is highly unlikely to be filed under 'G' in most record shops.

THE PROS AND CONS OF HITCH HIKING

HARVEST CDP 7 46029 2;
ORIGINALLY HARVEST SHVL 24 0105 1,
RELEASED: MAY 8 1984

Tracks: 4.30am (Apparently They Were Travelling Abroad); 4.33am (Running Shoes); 4.37am (Arabs With Knives And West German Skies) 4.39am (For The First Time Today Part 2); 4.41am (Sexual Revolution); 4.47am(The Remains Of Our Love); 4.30am (Go Fishing); 4.56am (For The First Time Today Part 1); 4.58am (Dunroamin, Duncarin, Dunlivin); 5.01am (The Pros And Cons Of Hitch Hiking); 5.06am (Every Strangers Eyes); 5.11am (The Moment of Clarity)

Waters' first solo album was a development of the demo of another concept offered to the band at the same time as 'The Wall', but rejected as "too personal". All the tracks were "time-stamped", representing the stages of the narrator's dream during one night, including picking up a hitch hiker, meeting Yoko Ono, having an affair in a German hotel, being attacked by terrorists, retiring to the country, being left by his wife and finally, waking to the realisation that his wife is by his side and all is well. Gerald Scarfe's sleeve, featuring a well known porn model, attracted complaints of sexism.

The album was recorded with Andy Bown (late of 'The Wall' concerts, keyboards and guitars), Ray Cooper (percussion), Michael Kamen (piano, orchestral arrangements and co-production, with Waters), Andy Newmark (drums), David Sanborn (sax) plus backing vocalists Madeline Bell, Katie Kissoon and Doreen Chanter, and horns from Raf Ravenscroft and others. Several actors also had spoken parts. However, by far the most notable member of the cast was Eric Clapton. Asked by a DJ what Clapton's contribution to the album was, Waters replied with a sarcastic "he played guitar!". That is something of an understatement, as Clapton's playing is widely regarded as his best for many years, relieved as he was of the burden of leading a band. He performs wonderfully emotional, bluesy passages, including some on Dobro.

Waters went on the road with Clapton, Kamen, Newmark, Kissoon and Chanter plus Tim Renwick (later to tour with Pink Floyd) and Mel Collins. Clapton was replaced after about twenty dates by Andy Fairweather-Low and Jay Stapley. The whole album was performed with back-projected films (including new Scarfe animation), costumed backing singers and puppets. Audiences also had the chance to hear Clapton play several Floyd classics, such as 'Money', the three short songs from 'Wish You Were Here', 'In The Flesh', 'Hey You' and 'Brain Damage'/'Eclipse'.

'5.01am (The Pros And Cons of Hitch Hiking)' was the album's first single (Harvest HAR 5228), backed by '4.30am (Apparently They Were Travelling Abroad)'. The 12" version (Harvest 12 HAR 5228) also included '4.33am (Running Shoes)' and an extended version of '5.01am (The Pros And Cons of Hitch Hiking)', with an alternative Eric Clapton guitar solo and extra saxophone.

A second single, '5.06am (Every Strangers Eyes)' (Harvest HAR 5230), backed by '4.39am (For The First Time Today Part 1)', was very hard to find and is something of a collectors' item.

WHEN THE WIND BLOWS
VIRGIN CDV2406 (CD),
RELEASED: OCTOBER 1986
CBS FOX 5156 (VIDEO)

Tracks: The Russian Missile; Towers Of Faith; Hilda's Dream; The American Bomber; The Anderson Shelter; The British Submarine; The Attack; The Fall Out; Hilda's Hair; Folded Flags

Waters wrote and produced the score of the animated feature film version of Raymond Briggs' graphic novel, directed by Jimmy T. Murakami. The first half of the album is by other artists.

The score, indexed on CD as one track, is all-instrumental, apart from 'Towers Of Faith' and 'Folded Flags'. The former, a duet with Clare Torry, is not heard in the movie, but was intended to be played in the auditorium as the lights went down, while the latter is a duet between Waters and Paul Carrack. The album credits the recording to "Roger Waters And The Bleeding Heart Band", which included Jay Stapley and Mel Collins, plus new faces Matt Irving and Nick Glennie Smith (both on keyboards), John Linwood (programming), Freddie Krc (drums) and John Gordon (bass).

RADIO KAOS
EMI CDP 7 46865 2;
ORIGINALLY HARVEST KAOS 1,
RELEASED: JUNE 15 1987

Tracks: Radio Waves; Who Needs Information; Me Or Him; The Powers That Be; Sunset Strip; Home; Four Minutes; The Tide Is Turning (After Live Aid)

'Radio KAOS' had a much more modern sound, which Waters has since regretted, but is still a powerful album. Its complicated plot required an explanation to be included in the sleeve notes; telling the unlikely tale of Billy, a telepathic paraplegic with the ability to communicate by telephone and computer. Eventually, Billy simulates a nuclear war in order to frighten the world into disarmament. Waters' story also includes attacks on

"market forces" and the way in which the fact that "information is power" disenfranchises so many people. Even so, the album ends on a high note, which, as its subtitle suggests, was written the day after the Live Aid concerts, to convey Waters' hopes for the future.

The album, co-produced with keyboard player Ian Ritchie (and Nick Griffiths on two tracks), was recorded by a basic band of Fairweather-Low, Collins, Jay Stapley and Graham Broad (drums) with many others contributing, including vocals by Paul Carrack, Clare Torry, Vicky Brown and the Pontarddulais Male Voice Choir. 'The Powers That Be' was performed by most of the line up that recorded the When The Wind Blows score, betraying its ancestry. The tracks were linked by conversations between Billy's BBC Micro computer generated voice and DJ Jim Ladd. In America, radio stations were issued with a promotional LP from which most of the dialogue between Jim Ladd and Billy had been removed.

The first single, 'Radio Waves (7" version)' (EMI EM 6) was backed by 'Going To Live In LA', a demo of a track not used on Radio KAOS. The 12" and CD singles had an additional re-mix of 'Radio Waves'. The second single, 'The Tide Is Turning' (EMI EM 37) boasted a "live" version of 'Money'; in reality a home studio recording with dubbed-on audience - Waters' bitter comment on his former band's continued success. The 12" and CD versions also included 'Get Back To Radio', also a demo not used on Radio KAOS. Another non-album track, 'Molly's Song', was featured on the US single 'Who Needs Information' (Columbia 38-07617) after being performed as part of the KAOS concerts.

Waters followed the album with a video EP, directed by Willie Smax, featuring promo clips for 'Radio Waves'; 'Sunset Strip'; 'Four Minutes' and 'The Tide Is Turning'. The recent reissue (Music Club MC 2128) omitted the explanatory liner notes of the original.

Both Carrack (playing keyboards and singing) and Ladd joined the basic band plus Chanter and Kissoon on a tour to promote the album. The shows, with additional KAOS material and Pink Floyd songs interspersed, were presented in the format of a radio show, with the band playing songs introduced by a DJ. During the interval, fans could "phone-in" from a booth in the auditorium and interview Waters. On some nights Waters would be gig-

ging in one American town while Pink Floyd played some of the same songs in another. A promised live album from the tour never materialised.

THE WALL LIVE IN BERLIN
MERCURY 846 611 2,
RELEASED: SEPTEMBER 17 1990
VIDEO: POLYGRAM MUSIC VIDEO 082 648-3

Tracks: In The Flesh?; The Thin Ice; Another Brick In The Wall (Part 1); The Happiest Days Of Our Lives; Another Brick In The Wall (Part 2); Mother; Goodbye Blue Sky; Empty Spaces; Young Lust; One Of My Turns; Don't Leave Me Now; Another Brick In The Wall (Part 3); Goodbye Cruel World; Hey You; Is There Anybody Out There?; Nobody Home; Vera; Bring The Boys Back Home; Comfortably Numb; In The Flesh; Run Like Hell; Waiting For The Worms; Stop; The Trial; The Tide Is Turning

On July 21 1990, Waters kept his promise to perform 'The Wall' in Berlin, if the real Berlin Wall ever came down. This meant he had to suspend work on a new opera called 'Ça Ira' ("We'll Make It"), intended to mark the Bi-centenary of the storming of the Bastille. At the invitation of French author Etienne Roda-Gil, who had written the libretto, Waters composed music for orchestra and singers. The celebration's organisers balked at the cost, and the project remains, as yet, unperformed and unrecorded.

The site of the 'Wall' concert was Potsdamer Platz, until recently a mined part of no-man's-land, but before then the heart of the old city. The concert was intended to raise funds for The Memorial Fund For Disaster Relief, a charity established by World War Two veteran Leonard Cheshire to raise £5 for every life lost in the wars of this century, to fund emergency aid programmes. Waters was joined by an impressive list of celebrities, including Bryan Adams; The Band (Levon Helm, Rick Danko and Garth Hudson); Paul Carrack; Tim Curry; Thomas Dolby; Marianne Faithfull; Albert Finney; James Galway; Jerry Hall; The Hooters; Cyndi Lauper; Ute Lemper; Joni Mitchell; Paddy Moloney; Van Morrison; Sinead O'Connor; and The Scorpions, plus The Military Orchestra of the Soviet Army and The East Berlin Radio Orchestra and Choir, all orchestrated and conducted by Michael Kamen.

Although credited, 'Empty Spaces' was not performed, Waters instead opting to sing 'What Shall We Do Now' at this point, just as he did during the original 'Wall' concerts. In order to end positively, Waters substituted 'The Tide Is Turning' for 'Outside The Wall'.

The album spawned two singles, 'Another Brick In The Wall (Part Two)' (Mercury MER 332) and the very rare 'The Tide Is Turning' (MER 336). Both were edited versions, with album versions added to 12" and CD formats. 'Another Brick...' also boasted a live version of 'Run Like Hell' on the 7" and an atypical, studio-reworked 'Potsdamer Mix' of it on other formats. 'The Tide Is Turning' was backed by 'Nobody Home' from the same concert.

The video has also been available on a '2 on 1' video with Pink Floyd's 'The Wall' movie (Polygram Video 087 730 3).

Although the concert was a massive spectacle, and all profits went to the charity, the resulting record – the only album of Waters' short relationship with Mercury – and video are disappointing. The best advice is to go and buy a copy, in order to support the charity, then go home and play the original instead.

AMUSED TO DEATH
COLUMBIA COL 4 68761 2,
RELEASED: SEPTEMBER 7 1992

Tracks: The Ballad Of Bill Hubbard; What God Wants, Part I; Perfect Sense, Part I; Perfect Sense, Part II; The Bravery Of Being Out Of Range; Late Home Tonight, Part I; Late Home Tonight, Part II; Too Much Rope; What God Wants, Part II; What God Wants, Part III; Watching TV; Three Wishes; It's A Miracle; Amused To Death

Waters worked, on and off, on this album for at least five years, originally announcing that it would be a continuation of the story-line of 'Radio KAOS'. In early 1989, EMI announced that a planned release had been abandoned, stressing that this was only because Waters himself was unhappy with it, and promising a release "by early 1990". In the end, the album was released by Columbia – now a part of the Sony conglomerate, not an EMI subsidiary as it was when Pink Floyd recorded for them in the Sixties.

The plot was even more complicated than that of 'Radio KAOS', and would justify a book of this length all to itself, but no explanatory notes were provided, and the dearth of contemporary interviews has not helped. Basically, the story, which takes its title from Neil Postman's book *Amusing Ourselves To Death*, revolves around the "Soap Opera State" where more attention is paid to politicians' hair styles, suits, sex-lives and television manner than their policies. References were also made to the bombing of Libya by US planes based in England, the Tiananmen Square massacre, terrorist atrocities and the discovery of the remains of the extinct Human species by alien anthropologists.

The album was dedicated to Private William Hubbard, whose colleague Alf Razzell was heard during the album's opening number, describing (on a television documentary) Hubbard's death in World War One. Waters again resorted to using lists for lyrics, but his worst sin was the stereotypical and sexist description of a Chinese dissident, his "yellow rose", as though her death only mattered because she was good looking.

Several numbers were graced by Jeff Beck, prompting Yardbirds fans to wonder when Waters will record with Jimmy Page.

Among the album's famous names were P.P. Arnold, John 'Rabbit' Bundrick, Rita Coolidge, N'Dea Davenport, Don Henley, Steve Lukather and Jeff Porcaro. A host of other musicians were also used, including old friends such as Michael Kamen, Andy Fairweather-Low, Graham Broad, Rick Di Fonzo, B.J. Cole, Katie Kissoon and Doreen Chanter, although Guy Pratt thought it politic to turn down an invitation to play bass! Surprisingly, Waters mostly restricts himself to vocals, playing only a very little bass, acoustic guitar or synthesiser.

Waters was sufficiently bitter, when Bob Ezrin pulled out of the 'Radio KAOS' to work on 'Momentary Lapse' instead, to include the lyric "Each man has his price, Bob/and yours was pretty low". Patrick Leonard stepped into the void, co-producing with Waters, and also contributed keyboards. A multitude of studios were used, including The Billiard Room at Waters' London home, Compass Point in Nassau, Abbey Road, and eight others in London and the US.

After performing 'What God Wants' at The Guitar Legends festival in Seville and a charity concert in the US, Waters announced that he would tour with the album if it sold two million copies. Twelve months after its release, it had sold just over half that figure.

Again, two singles were released. 'What God Wants, Part I (Video Edit)' (Columbia 658 139) came on 7", cassette and two CD formats, the second CD being in a box with colour prints taken from the promo video. There was no 12" release. The extra tracks were all from the album, as were all the tracks on the various formats of the second single, 'The Bravery Of Being Out Of Range' (658 819).

richard wright

WET DREAM

HARVEST SHVL 818 (UK VINYL);
SONY A24090 (USA CD),
RELEASED: SEPTEMBER 22 1978

Tracks: Mediterranean C; Against The Odds; Cat Cruise; Summer Elegy; Waves; Holiday; Mad Yannis Dance; Drop In From The Top; Pink's Song; Funky Deux

For his first solo album, Richard Wright took Gilmour's advice and went to Superbear, where he made this often overlooked, if somewhat bland, record, accompanied by top session musicians Mel Collins (sax) Snowy White (guitar), Larry Steele (bass) and Reg Isadore (drums). The sleeve was by Hipgnosis. No singles were released from the album, and Wright did not perform any concerts.

The lyrics to 'Pink's Song' (not 'Against The Odds', as stated on the US CD credits) were written by Wright's then wife, Juliette,

who as Juliette Gale, was a singer with an early incarnation of Pink Floyd, The Abdabs. Appearances are not what they seem; the song is actually about their children's tutor, who happened to share his nickname with the "star" of 'The Wall'.

IDENTITY (as Zee)

HARVEST SHSP 24 0101 1 (NOT ON CD),
RELEASED: APRIL 9 1984

Tracks: Confusion; Voices; Private Person; Strange Rhythm; Cuts Like A Diamond; By Touching; How Do You Do It; Seems We Were Dreaming; Eyes Of A Gypsy' (on cassette only)

After leaving Pink Floyd, Wright formed a short-lived partnership, called Zee, with Dave Harris, former leader of New Romantic band Fashion, with Wright composing music for Harris' lyrics. The album bears much more resemblance to Fashion than anything produced by Pink Floyd. There were again no live dates. This is the only Floyd solo album never released on CD anywhere.

'Confusion' was issued as a single, backed by 'Eyes Of A Gypsy' (Harvest HAR 5227). The 12" had an extended mix of the A-side and a dub version of the B-side (12 HAR 5227).

index

Bold page numbers indicate descriptive entry; solo material not included.

10/02 (45673)